happy stitch

Jodie Rackley

NORTH LIGHT BOOKS

CINCINNATI, OHIO

table of contents

Introduction

I create to make others smile and to remind them of the bright side of life. So often in our modern, fast-paced times we forget to slow down and cherish all the wonderful things around us. This is one of the reasons I fell fast for embroidery and hand sewing. Sure, it takes a little more time and a bit more effort, but with some patience you'll learn to slow down and enjoy the process.

Until a few years ago, I had always been more of a painter and sketcher. My new love for embroidery all began with a needle, thread and a simple knot. I began "drawing" doodles with my needle and thread, creating a fun, colorful picture in thread. Sewing is now part of my everyday life—stitching endlessly in my studio for my product line, Lova Revolutionary.

Embroidery and hand sewing have such a delightful, calming effect. You can take it with you almost anywhere or stitch a bit while watching your favorite show as you transform your own drawings into sewn creations. I fall into my own little happy zone and let all of my cares and worries drift away. My favorite pieces to create are much more detailed works. Even though it's not instant gratification, there's such a fantastic feeling of accomplishment in seeing a thousand little stitches become a masterpiece! The best part is that it's so simple. Even with the most basic stitches (all which you'll learn here), we'll make our stitched masterpieces come to life.

When I place my projects around my home, I remember the time spent making them and every tiny stitch it took to complete them. These curious little touches are what every home should have—pieces that start conversations, add texture, color and whimsy, and help spread happiness. Whether we're making everyday gifts, keepsakes for special occasions or stitching up unique designs to use in our homes, handmade goodies allow us to share a little bit of our hearts and crafty souls with others.

I designed these projects in the hopes that you could bring a smile to your space and world, and I really hope that you enjoy them! We'll be using basic embroidery stitches and some simple sewing to craft everything from softies to place mats to gadget cozies. There's a little something for everyone inside, and almost anyone with a bit of crafty skill will be able to work each project. I encourage you to add your own touches of flair and personality to truly make these your own. Happy stitching!

XOXO,

Jodie

Supplies

Felt: You can choose from a variety of felts at almost any craft store, including ecospun felt, wool felt and standard acrylic felt, plus many blends in between. For the majority of projects in this book, I used ecospun felt because I adore the bold colors, variety and texture—plus it's recycled! Feel free to use any blend of felt that you'd like. They are all easy to work with and to embroider. You can find felt in sheets for smaller projects and in yardage for larger projects.

Scissors: A variety of different types of scissors is a must for any crafter. While most projects can be made with just a standard pair, it really makes crafting easier to have different tools to accomplish different tasks. When working with felt, a sharp, fine-tip pair of detail scissors is best for cutting out small pieces. They're also great for cutting around templates. A pair of sewing shears (the type that lay flat on one side) is perfect for cutting out pieces from your fabric yardage and for making patchworks. Generally, sewing shears are very sharp to keep the fabric from pulling or getting caught while cutting. It's also good to have a pair of pinking shears which cut in a zigzag pattern. They are fun to use for decorative fabric edges and for finishing seams so they do not fray. Finally, you'll need a standard pair of craft scissors for cutting out paper templates.

Fabric and Interfacing: You can embroider and sew on almost any type of fabric. Since many of the projects in this book are functional items as well as decorative, I recommend using heavier cottons or lightweight denims, since both provide a durable and sturdy surface on which to sew by hand or machine. Blended cottons and polyesters can pull, stretch and fray if you're not careful when hand sewing. If you use lightweight cottons or blends, apply fusible interfacing to the wrong side of the fabric. This thin webbing provides extra strength to the fabric and will help keep it from pulling, stretching or fraying when you're working with it. When sewing together bold prints, place a layer of fusible interfacing or muslin in between the two pieces of fabric to prevent the pattern or stitching from showing through to the other side.

Floss: Embroidery floss can be found as individual color skeins at almost any craft store. It is available in many different varieties such as cotton, linen, metallic, variegated and even glow-in-the-dark. Embroidery floss is made of six individual threads twisted together to make a thick thread. Most floss by major manufacturers is also coded with a specific number that is interchangeable between different brands. If you use up a certain color before finishing your design, this numbering systems allows you to easily find the same color again. You can also keep your floss organized by using floss bobbins to store your thread and by noting the color number on the bobbin; this also helps to keep your floss from getting tangled. Split embroidery floss by pulling the different strands apart, and use two or three strands instead of all six for finer detail work or a softer look.

Embroidery Hoops: Embroidery hoops can be functional as well as decorative and come in a variety of sizes to fit your needs. They can be made out of wood, plastic or metal, but for the projects in this book, we will use wooden embroidery hoops available at most craft stores. Hoops are a must for working on larger embroidery motifs. They keep the fabric taut and in place and allow you to clearly see your working surface. Hoops can also be used as frames for finished embroidery or patchwork pieces.

Sewing Machine and Thread: For the projects in this book, any standard sewing machine will do. While the majority of projects in this book use hand-sewing techniques, a few of the more complicated projects will require a sewing machine. But don't worry—only basic sewing skills are required and any standard thread will work just fine.

Adhesives: A basic craft glue will work well for most craft projects. Felt glue is perfect for gluing felt to felt or felt to fabric since it is usually a little less runny than standard craft glue. Clear fabric glue is necessary for gluing fabric onto other surfaces.

Stuffing: Stuff your softies and add dimension to many of your felt projects with a standard acrylic stuffing, available at craft stores. While the texture can vary between different brands of stuffing, most will yield the same results. A stuffing that is less silky and more cottonlike is best for filling softies and for use with smaller projects. Silky stuffing is more difficult to ball up and the texture can make it a bit slippery to work with, especially when creating smaller stuffed items.

Techniques

French Seams: French seams are a nice and easy way to enclose your seam so that it is finished on both sides of the piece, especially when the seam will be visible when finished. French seams look professional and are super easy to do! To sew a French seam, place two fabrics wrong sides together. Sew the fabrics together, staying about ¼" (6mm) away from the edge. Trim the seam allowance a little closer to the stitches if you'd like and turn the piece inside out so that the wrong sides are facing out. Press down the edge with an iron and stitch along the outside edge again about ½" (13mm) from the edge. Turn the piece right side out and your seam will be enclosed both inside and out.

Stuffing Tips: While stuffing a pillow, softie or ornament seems quite easy, there is actually a bit of a trick to stuffing your project fully and evenly. Begin by pulling the stuffing apart and pushing small pieces into any small details or points in your project. Use your finger tip, a chopstick or the eraser end of a pencil to push small pieces of stuffing into the little nooks and crannies of the piece. Once all of the points and details are stuffed, continue pushing small pieces of stuffing into the outside edges, working all the way around the piece. Once all of the edges and points are firmly stuffed, add larger pieces to the middle until the piece is fully stuffed. Once you've stuffed up to the hole, add a bit more stuffing so that when your edge is sewn together, there will not be any looseness in the edge where your last seam will be.

Using Templates: Templates are an easy way to cut your felt uniformly and precisely. Simply enlarge your templates onto cardstock or heavyweight paper and cut them out. Since felt is difficult to mark on, these will become your patterns. Using thicker paper allows you to reuse the template over and over again. Pin the template directly to the felt using one or more pins if necessary. Using your template as a guide, slowly cut closely around the outside edge of the template. Remove the pins and template to reveal a nicely cut felt shape.

Transferring Embroidery Designs: The easiest way to transfer your embroidery design to your fabric is to use a simple carbon transfer paper. It generally comes in a pack of a few sheets and will have two different colors—one light color and one dark color. Use the darker color for transferring to lighter fabrics and the light color for transferring to darker fabrics. Begin by layering your pieces of paper and fabric. Place the fabric right side up on a hard, smooth surface. Place the transfer paper right side down on top of the fabric. On top, place the copied design right side up. Using a ball point pen, trace over your design, pressing firmly so that the design transfers thoroughly. If the design is still too faint in color, trace over it again to make it darker and thicker. Remove the design and transfer paper to reveal your design. Embroider directly over your design. When you are finished embroidering, remove any remaining lines by gently rubbing over them with a clean pencil eraser.

9

Embroidery Stitches

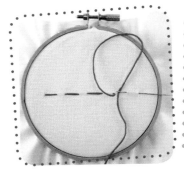  

Straight Stitch: To make a straight stitch, pull your needle through from the wrong side of the fabric and back down through the right side. Leave a space and repeat, coming up through the bottom and down through the top.

Backstitch: To make a backstitch, first make a single straight stitch. Leave a small space and pull the thread back up through to the top of the fabric. Then stitch down through the end where the straight stitch stopped.

Star Stitch: To make a star stitch, first make a straight stitch going from north to south. Then make another stitch going from east to west, followed by two more straight stitches at the points in between.

Cross Stitch: To make a cross stitch, simply make two straight stitches that form an X shape. Place them far apart or close together by stitching back through the holes from your previous stitch.

Blanket Stitch: To make a blanket stitch, insert your needle halfway through the back side of the piece. Once it is halfway through, take the hanging thread and loop it over your needle counterclockwise. Once looped, finish pulling your needle completely through the piece. Bring your needle once again halfway through the back side of the piece, loop the hanging thread counterclockwise, and finish pulling through your piece. Continue to repeat. Always work your blanket stitch counterclockwise, moving from the left to the right of the piece. This is an easy edging stitch that you can use to securely close the edge of plushies, pillows and anything you'd like to finish with a decorative edge.

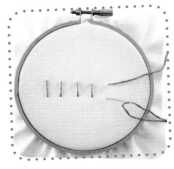

Appliqué Stitch: To make an appliqué stitch, insert your needle from the back side at the top edge of the item you wish to appliqué. Make a single stitch over the top edge and down through your appliqué piece. Repeat along the entire outside edge of your appliqué, following the edge or curvature of your piece. You can also use the appliqué stitch to close an outside edge. To use it as an edging stitch: Stitch through from the back side, loop over your edge, and bring your needle through the back side again, repeating until your edge is finished.

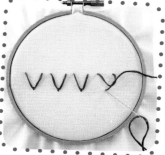

Open Loop Stitch: To make an open loop stitch, insert your needle from the back side of your piece, and bring your thread all the way through and back down through the top of your piece. Pull your thread most of the way through, leaving a loop at the end of your thread; hold the loop in place with your finger if you need to. Bring your needle through from the back side through the loop, pulling the thread all the way through so that the loop is tightly in place. Stitch down through the top very close to the bottom of the loop so there is a small stitch holding the bottom of the loop in place.

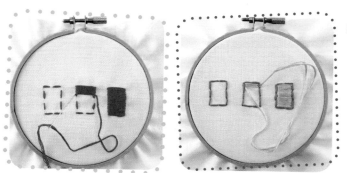

Fill Stitch: To make a raised fill stitch, outline the area you'd like to fill with a straight or backstitch. Then pull your needle up through the bottom near the outside edge of the area. Straight stitch down through the other outside edge of your fill stitch. Continue stitching closely together until your entire shape is completely filled. If there are still places where the fabric is showing through, simply stitch over the entire top of that area. Sometimes you may want to add an outline or more color—in this case, work your fill stitch on the inside edges of your outline stitch for a different look. Using the same method, pull your thread through from the back near the inside edge of your outline stitch and down through the opposite edge on the inside, working until you've filled the shape.

Personalize It

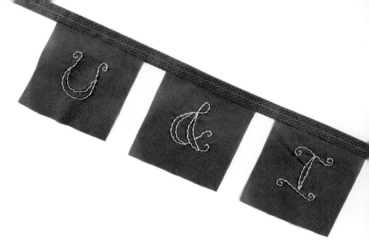

Bringing little personal touches to your projects is easy with these simple techniques. Learn to incorporate your own handwriting, make silhouettes and place simple monograms on your projects. These methods will add a custom touch to your work and help make it your own.

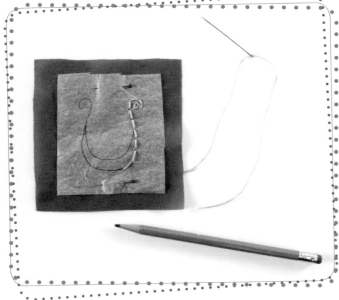

Creating Stitched Handwriting: All you will need is paper, white tissue or tracing paper, needle and thread, and the fabric or surface you wish to work on. Write out your handwritten letters or message on plain white paper. Place tissue paper over your message and trace it in pencil. Place the tracing paper onto the fabric or working surface, and pin it in place. With a needle and thread, backstitch through your fabric and tracing paper over your design. When you're finished, gently pull the tissue paper away from the stitches. This is also a great way to stitch very small details or small lettering that uses thinner pieces of thread. Instead of handwriting, you can also use your favorite font for a more uniform look. This is also a great way to preserve children's drawings and early writing!

Making Silhouettes: Find your favorite profile photo of your subject. Print out or photocopy the photo, making it as large or small as you'd like. I recommend at least 6"–8" (15.2cm to 20.3cm) for the height of your silhouette. Once you have your profile printed out, trace along the edge of the larger details with a black marker. Cut out the silhouette to use as a template. Pin it to felt or fabric and cut around all the edges using small detail scissors. Glue the silhouette to another piece of fabric or paper for framing, or appliqué stitch it to a project of your choice.

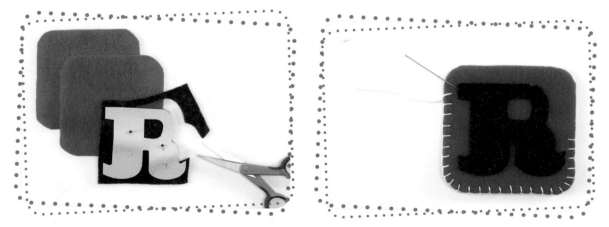

Monograms: Choose your favorite large or bold font. Size your letters the desired size in your publishing program on your computer. Print the letters onto cardstock and cut around the edges to make your templates. Pin the templates to felt and cut around the edges using detail scissors. I glued my monograms with felt glue onto a square of felt and used a blanket stitch around the edge to create some fun coasters.

Über-Cute Projects for the Crafty Life

Handmade goodies don't always have to be a piece of art or a decorative item. We should carry a bit of craftiness everywhere we go, and making fun and funky, cute and whimsical accessories will help us do just that. Stitched projects for your home enhance the charm and warmth of your space while adding extra visual interest that family and guests will love. You'll be surprised how one neatly crafted piece can really change the look and feel of your space. And don't forget that everybody adores gifts made with love! They always seem to be the pieces that fill our treasure boxes and keepsake drawers. Have fun making these über-cute projects to wear out on the town, decorate your space or give to someone special in your life.

Owl Gadget Cozy

Handheld gadgets are the ultimate accessory. We carry them with us wherever we go, and they help us capture those fun moments in life—calling our best friend from a road trip, sending a smiling snapshot to family or jamming to our favorite tunes. Why not give your gadget a little retro-inspired friend to keep it safe and cozy? Crafted out of colorful felt, patterned fabric and simple hand embroidery, these groovy owls are one of my most popular designs and the perfect size to fit most phones, MP3 players and cameras. These owls have been flying all over the globe to people far and wide, and now they're ready to journey with you, too!

Supplies:

- templates (page 132) • cardboard or cardstock • 5 colors of felt (body, wing, eyes, beak, white)
- 1 patterned fabric • 3 colors of embroidery floss (body, eyes, beak) • embroidery needle
- scissors • pins

Row House Tablet/ eReader Cozies

Get your reader or tablet ready to hit the streets with this fancy row-house-inspired cozy. Made with mix-and-match templates and easy stitches, you can create your own neighborhood of cozies for all your gadgets.

Supplies:

- templates (page 132) • cardboard or cardstock • 2 sheets of felt for the house • a variety of felt for the appliqués • fabric for lining • several colors of embroidery floss • embroidery needle • scissors • pins • tape measure or ruler

Instructions for the Owl Gadget Cozy

1 Photocopy, enlarge and cut out all of the templates from heavy paper. Cut a body front and back from one color of felt and a body front and back from patterned fabric. From a second color of felt, cut out the right wing shape and brow. Cut the left wing shape from patterned fabric. Using the circle templates, cut two large white felt circles and two small contrasting felt circles for the eyes. Cut a beak from another color of felt.

2 Pin the fabric wing on the left side of the felt body front, and start an appliqué stitch at the top of the wing close to the edge. Stitch along the rounded edge. When you come to the end of the rounded edge, straight stitch along the inside of the wing until you reach the bottom of the cozy. Knot the thread to finish.

3 Place the felt wing on the right side, overlapping the fabric wing. Beginning at the bottom, appliqué stitch the inside edge of the wing. Then use open loop stitches (as large as you'd like) to cover the wing and give the illusion of feathers. (I used six large loop stitches.)

4 Center the felt brow shape at the top of the cozy. Stitch it in place using five appliqué stitches—two on each side and one in the center. Next, stack the large and small circles for the eyes. Using a straight stitch and matching embroidery floss for the eye color, secure each eye in place. Center the small diamond shape between the eyes for the owl's beak and secure it with a star stitch.

5 Place the completed front together with the patterned fabric, wrong sides together. Blanket stitch along the top of the cozy, working from left to right. Once you complete the last stitch, knot and tie off the thread between the layers of felt and fabric.

6 Layer the felt body back with the lining fabric and pin together. Layer all of the pieces together with the right sides of the lining fabric facing each other and with the felt pieces forming the front and back of the cozy. Blanket stitch from the bottom center of the cozy all the way around. Once you reach the starting point, loop the hanging thread through the first stitch, slip the thread through the center of the cozy and out the back, then knot and tie it. Voilà! You made a cute and wise owl to carry your gadgets.

More Stitchery Ideas
Try modifying the cozy by adding another half-size felt piece on the back to create a pouch for head-phones or cards. Or sew a small felt rectangle on the back, stitched at both ends, to make a loop for your belt. Use buttons for eyes instead of felt for a totally different look.

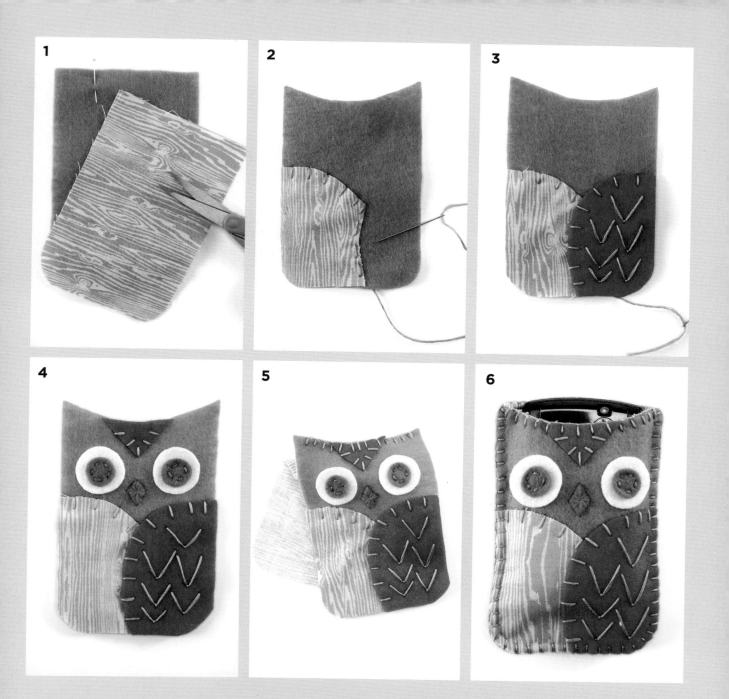

Instructions for the Row House Tablet/eReader Cozies

1 To make the main part of the house, cut two 8″ x 10″ (20.3cm x 25.4cm) rectangles from a felt sheet. (This is the perfect size for the iPad. Scale your measurements and templates down a few inches for smaller eReaders like Nook or Kindle.) Cut two lining rectangles the same size from the coordinating fabric. Stack all four rectangles and use scissors to round the corners on one of the short sides. From the templates on page 132, choose a roof, door and windows for the house. Photocopy, enlarge and cut out all of the templates from heavy paper.

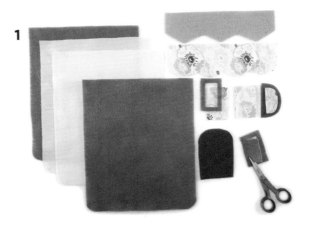

Cut out two roof shapes (one out of felt and one out of fabric). Trim the width of one down a bit so it is narrower than the other. Using the window template, cut as many windows as you'd like out of contrasting felt. To cut window panes, pinch the felt together and make a small cut at the fold to start; continue cutting small squares in the felt windows until you have as many panes as you'd like. Use the window template again to cut pieces of fabric to go behind the pane to represent glass or curtains.

2 Line up the roof pieces at the top of the cozy and appliqué or straight stitch the bottom edge of each. Place the window panes with the fabric behind them; then use an appliqué or straight stitch to sew them in place. Use a straight stitch to sew on the door, and add a felt circle doorknob using a star stitch.

3 With wrong sides together, pin one lining rectangle to each half of the felt cozy, aligning the edges. Blanket stitch from left to right across the top of the back half of the house, stitching through both the house and lining fabric. Knot and tie on the lining side.

4 Match up the front and back halves of the cozy, felt sides out. Blanket stitch from the bottom middle of the cozy up to the top left corner. Continue sewing a blanket stitch along the front half of the cozy to the top right corner, and then continue stitching through all four layers until you reach the starting point.

5 Knot and tie the thread on the back side of the cozy when you are finished. Mix and match the templates to create a variety of cute and cozy little row houses.

More Stitchery Ideas
Use your imagination to cut out house embellishments from the felt and fabric (like doorknobs and door paneling). Try using a contrasting embroidery floss color for the stitching—it adds another special touch to the project.

2

3

4

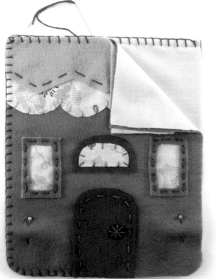

5

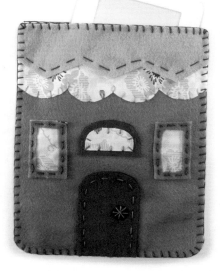

Monster Face Computer Covers

Too many unwanted guests on your computer? Let these cute and scary monsters guard them for you. Using a variety of felt and easy straight stitches, we'll make cute monster faces to use as laptop cases or screen covers. Mix and match the templates to create your own unique face, or follow my example as a guideline. The monsters will keep your computer safe and sound, all while making you smile!

Supplies:

• templates (page 132) • cardboard or cardstock • a variety of felt for face pieces • a large piece of felt for cover, ½ yard to 1 yard (0.5m to 0.9m) depending on size • several colors of embroidery floss • snap (if making a laptop case) • embroidery needle • scissors • pins • tape measure or ruler

Instructions for the Monster Face Computer Covers

1 Photocopy, enlarge and cut out all of the templates from heavy paper. Cut each of the face features you'd like to use out of the desired color of felt. Measure the height and width of your monitor or laptop and add 1"–2" (2.5cm to 5.1cm) to each measurement to allow for the thickness of the screen. Cut two felt pieces for a screen cover in the appropriate size, or cut four felt pieces for a laptop case.

2 Arrange the face templates on one felt rectangle and pin them in place. For best results, pin the eyes evenly and then arrange the other components. Stitch the face features in place. When shapes overlap, use a straight stitch to sew down the bottom shapes first; then arrange and stitch the top components. Match the floss colors to the felt for a more subtle look, or use contrasting floss for a bolder look. Add a few decorative stitches, such as a star stitch, if desired.

3 **If making a screen cover,** sew a straight stitch across the bottom on the front piece and again across the bottom on the back piece of felt. Next, pin the front and back together and sew a straight stitch along both sides and the top of the cover, leaving the bottom open. Trim the edges evenly, and slip the cover over your screen.

If making a laptop case, pin all four rectangular pieces of felt together so there are two for each side of the case. Straight stitch along both sides and the top of the case. Knot and tie on the back when finished.

4 To make the strap for the snap, cut two 5" x 2" (12.7cm x 5.1cm) pieces of felt. Toward the bottom of one of these pieces, sew the top piece of one small snap into place. Trim the corners on the end where you placed the snap so they are rounded. Pin the two pieces of felt together and straight stitch all the way around the edge.

5 Place the strap where you'd like it between the top two layers of the case and pin in place. Straight stitch across the bottom edge of the case, stitching the top two layers together and securing the strap in place. Now flip the case over. Using the strap as a guide, decide where you need to place the remaining snap piece, and sew it in place through both layers of back felt.

6 Once completed, sew a straight stitch across the bottom back of the case. Insert your laptop and snap in place.

1

2

3

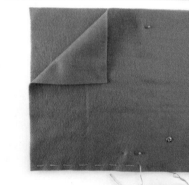

4

5

6

Chevron Headband

Accessories are an awesome way to add a little quirkiness to your everyday wardrobe. Make a headband with a sleek, modern vibe using felt, embroidery and a cool graphic design.

Supplies:

• templates (page 133) • cardboard or cardstock • 3 colors of felt and 1 color of stiffened felt • thin elastic cording • 1 color of matching embroidery floss • felt glue • heavy book • embroidery needle • scissors • pins

Funky Fascinator

Spruce up your next outfit with a cute fascinator! Make this one your own by mixing fabric, felt, lace, buttons, or any notions that you love to create a one-of-a-kind hair piece. Create a funky piece for everyday or a fancy fascinator for a wedding or party.

Supplies:

• templates (page 133) • cardboard or cardstock • 1 color of felt • 1 small piece of patterned fabric • variety of extra-funky notions (such as buttons, ribbon, rickrack, crochet flowers, lace) • 1 color of embroidery floss • 1 large hair clip • embroidery needle • scissors • pins

Instructions for the Chevron Headband

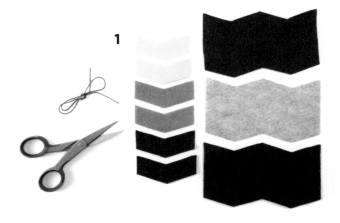

1

1 Photocopy, enlarge and cut out all of the templates from heavy paper. Cut two chevron arrow pieces out of three different colors of felt. Cut two base pieces out of one color of matching felt and cut one base piece out of stiffened felt.

2 Apply felt glue all the way around the edge and in lines through the center of one matching felt base piece. (Use the glue sparingly, as it may seep through to the top if applied too thickly.) Begin placing the chevron pieces on top of the base so that the edges match up evenly. I varied my colors in each row to create a staggered chevron look. Press the chevrons firmly in place and allow to dry for about an hour.

3 Once the pieces are dry and securely in place, add a few embroidery stitches in a V shape to the center seams of the chevron design.

4 Cut a piece of elastic cording long enough to stretch around the bottom of your head without being too tight. Tie a knot at both ends of the cording. Place one end of the cord vertically centered on one side of the stiffened felt base piece. Stitch around the cording on both sides of the knot to secure it in place. Continue stitching the cord close to the edge of the base. Repeat to attach the other side of elastic cording to the base piece.

5 Spread felt glue thoroughly over one side of the stiffened felt base piece. Glue the remaining felt base piece to the stiffened felt. Hold the pieces firmly until the glue starts to adhere.

6 Flip the piece over and repeat to adhere the chevron piece to the other side of the stiffened felt. Place a heavy book or object on top of the headband and let it dry overnight.

7 Put on your cutest outfit and wear it with style!

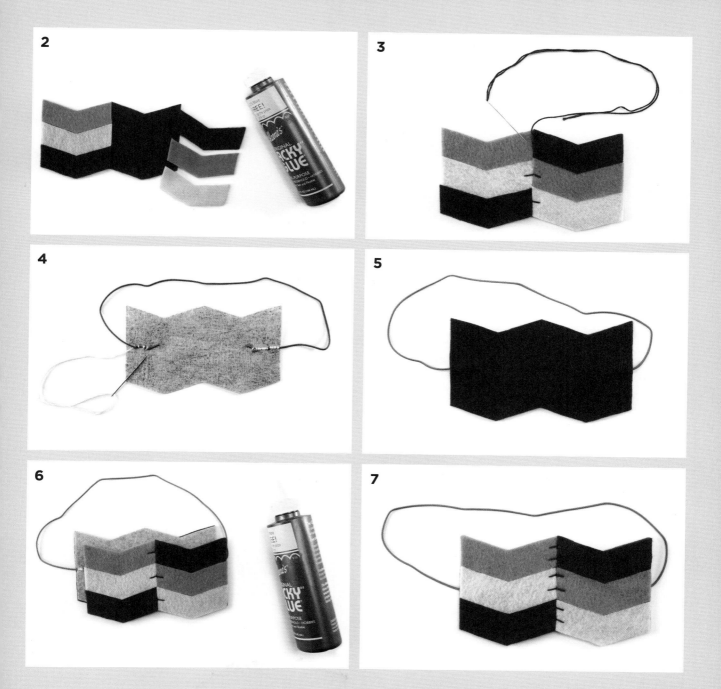

Instructions for the Funky Fascinator

1 Photocopy, enlarge and cut out all of the templates from heavy paper. Cut two large oval pieces out of felt and one small oval out of a patterned or accent fabric.

2 Center and pin the small fabric oval on top of one large felt oval. With embroidery floss, appliqué stitch all the way around the edge of the small oval. Knot and tie on the back side when you are finished. Now embellish the piece any way you'd like. Use simple embroidery stitches to secure any trims or notions. (For my piece, I used felt, crochet accents, lace and a few buttons. I left a little fabric showing for a splash of pattern and color.)

3 Next, attach the hair clip. (I used a spring clip but feel free to use the clip of your choice.) Position the spring clip on the back of the second felt oval and stitch it in place through both layers. (On my spring clip, I stitched through the hole on either end and around the middle of the clip several times.)

4 Gather up some fun ribbons, lace or rickrack to add some flair to the fascinator. Place the embellished oval on top of the second oval, and pin together at one end. Cut a few pieces of ribbon, lace or rickrack and place them in between the layers of felt. Work a straight stitch through all the felt layers, going all the way around the edge. (I started stitching where I placed the ribbons to secure those first before continuing around the rest of the oval.)

5 Knot and tie on the back when you are finished stitching. Wear and enjoy!

1

More Stitchery Ideas
Use this simple oval shape and a variety of crafty scraps to create and embellish fun hair pieces to make any occasion a little extra fancy. You can also use the instructions from the Chevron Headband project to turn this piece into a headband.

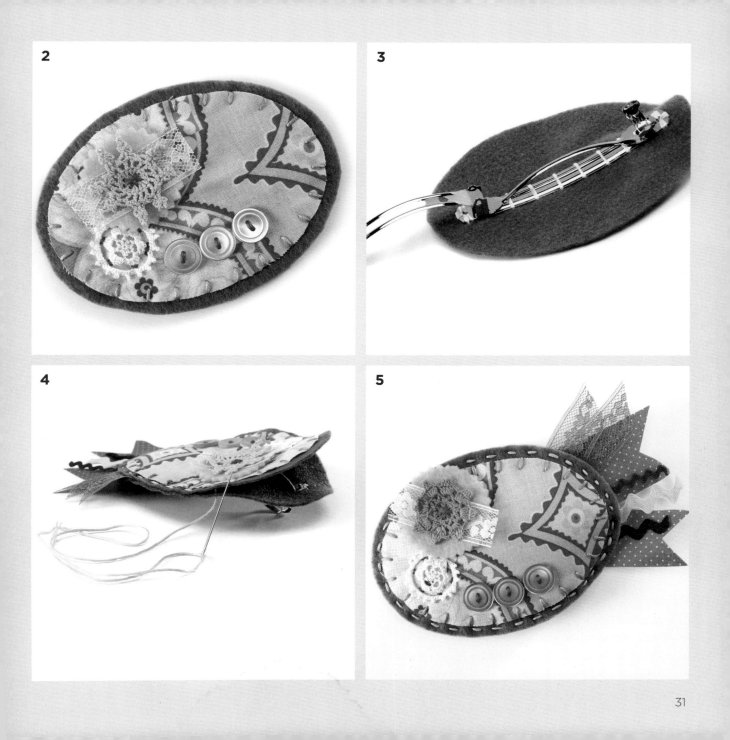

Mushroom Mini Bag

Accent your outfit with a bit of funky, fabulous fungus fashion. Meant to go with you everywhere, this sweet little bag can be worn two ways: Bring playfulness to your swagger by wearing it on your hip for easy access to your phone or keys, or as a shoulder bag to keep your camera and other go-to gadgets handy.

Supplies:

• templates (page 133) • cardboard or cardstock • 2 felt sheets for mushroom • 2 felt sheets for mushroom lining • felt for polka dots • fabric for mushroom top (small piece) and strap (long piece) • 2 colors of matching embroidery floss • embroidery needle • scissors • pins • tape measure or ruler • iron • sewing machine (optional)

Rainbow Card Case

Nothing brightens your day like a chance meeting with a rainbow on a summer afternoon. For this happy little card case, use many layers of brightly colored felt to create a bold rainbow design complete with a fluffy cloud.

Supplies:

• templates (page 133) • cardboard or cardstock • 6 different colors of felt (pink, blue or teal, green, purple, white and light blue/gray) • 4 colors of embroidery floss (pink, blue or teal, green and purple) • 1 sew-on snap • embroidery needle • scissors • pins • stuffing

Instructions for the Mushroom Mini Bag

1 Photocopy, enlarge and cut out all of the templates from heavy paper. From the felt sheets, cut two mushrooms for the outside of the purse and two for the lining. Cut one mushroom top out of fabric. Cut as many felt dots as you'd like. Cut a 2" (5.1cm) wide length of fabric for the strap, as long as you need to go around your waist plus about 6" (15.2cm) so you can tie it later. Pin the fabric mushroom top in place over the top of the felt mushroom and appliqué stitch along the bottom of the fabric mushroom top only. Add a few straight stitches to the bottom of the mushroom for extra flair.

2 Place and pin the felt dots on the fabric mushroom top. Straight stitch around the edge of each dot, leaving any parts that align with the outside edge free of stitches. Add additional embellishments, such as buttons or a felt butterfly, to the mushroom front.

3 To create the strap loops, cut two 2" × 4" (5.1cm × 10.2cm) pieces of fabric. Fold the long outside edges in to the center and iron flat. Fold each piece in half lengthwise again, lining up the ironed edges, and straight stitch along both sides with embroidery floss or a sewing machine. After stitching the long sides, fold each piece in half widthwise and pin them to the back mushroom piece. Cut two more felt dots and place them just over the raw ends of the loops. Leave enough loop exposed to fit the strap through. Straight stitch around the edges of the dots to hold the loops in place.

Next take the long strap piece, fold each short end under ½" (13mm) and iron flat. Fold the long sides in to the center and iron flat. Fold the strap in half again, matching the long edges, and iron in place. Stitch along the long sides in the same way you did for the loops.

4 With wrong sides together, pin one felt mushroom lining to the back mushroom piece. Blanket stitch across the top of the mushroom back, starting a few inches (or centimeters) above the bottom of the mushroom top and working from left to right. Knot and tie off when finished.

5 Pin the remaining felt mushroom lining to the back of the mushroom front. Then match up the front and back lined pieces, linings face each other. Blanket stitch through all four layers from the bottom to the top left corner. Then stitch only through the front piece and front lining across the top. Finally, stitch through all four layers from the top right corner until you reach the point where you started. Knot and tie on the back side when you are finished.

6 Slip the strap through the loops on the back of the purse. Tie the strap around your waist or knot the strap ends for a shoulder strap.

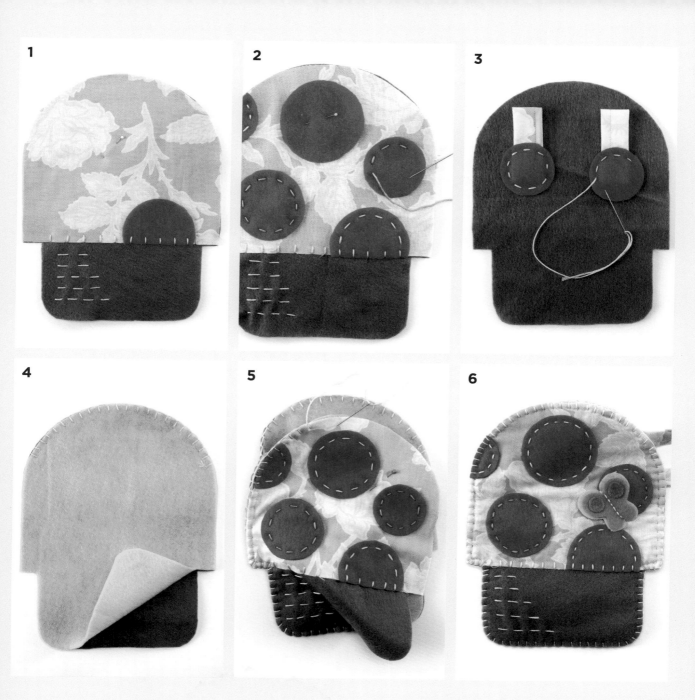

Instructions for the Rainbow Card Case

1 Photocopy, enlarge and cut out all of the templates from heavy paper. Cut two large arches out of pink felt and two out of light blue/gray felt (lining). Cut medium-large arch out of teal or blue felt. Cut one medium-small arch out of green felt, and cut one small arch out of purple felt. Cut one cloud piece out of white felt.

Place and pin the blue arch on top of the pink arch, making sure it's centered in the middle and even with the bottom of the pink piece. Using pink floss, straight stitch around the curve, leaving the bottom unstitched. In the same way, place and stitch the green arch over the blue using purple floss. Repeat to stitch on the purple arch with green floss.

2 Place and pin the cloud shape on top of the rainbow layers, aligning the bottom edges. Using blue floss, stitch along the top of the cloud. Knot and tie on the back side when you are finished.

3 From the light blue/gray felt, cut two small squares to reinforce the snap. Center the small square at the top of one lining piece, about ½" (13mm) from the top. Place the snap in the center of the small square on the back side so the square will not show in the finished piece. Stitch the snap in place through both layers, working through each hole several times. Repeat with the other snap piece on the other square and lining piece, making sure that the snaps line up properly. (To ensure proper snap placement, place the second lining piece on top of the finished piece with the right side down. Pull up the top edge to reveal the snap. When you reach the center of the snap, make a small dot on the incomplete piece with a pen or marker. This will help you sew the snap in the right place.)

4 Evenly pin one lining piece to the remaining pink arch piece. Straight stitch along the curve.

5 Pin the other lining piece on the back side of the rainbow. Layer the front section on top of the back section with linings together. Straight stitch through all four layers, from the top left corner and across the bottom. As you stitch along the bottom, lightly stuff the cloud. Continue stitching up the other side.

6 Once you reach the top right corner, continue stitching along the front section of the pouch only. When you reach the starting point, knot and tie the thread on the inside of the pouch. Stuff with your personal cards and you're in business.

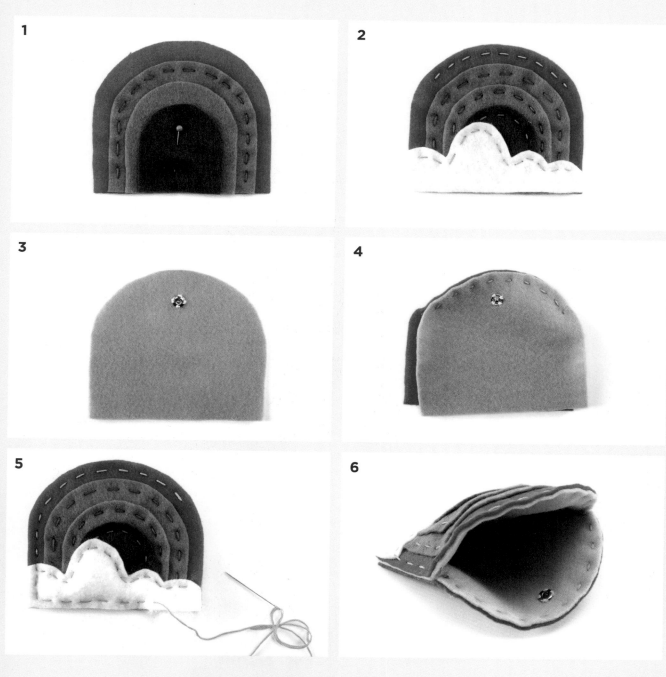

Embroidered Tote Bag

Spend some time creating detailed, hand-stitched embroideries inspired by the beautiful tradition of the Mexican dress. Fashion your lovely hand-stitched designs into wearable works of art by creating a go-to tote you can take anywhere.

Supplies:

- embroidery designs (page 134) • carbon tracing paper or transfer pencil • light-colored, small-patterned fabric: 2 bag pieces cut to 15″ x 14″ (38.1cm x 35.6cm), 2 strap pieces cut to 4″ x 30″ (10.2cm x 76.2cm) • 2 pieces of lining fabric, cut to 4″ x 30″ (10.2cm x 76.2cm)
- a variety of embroidery floss • 6″ or 8″ (15.2cm or 20.3cm) embroidery hoop
- embroidery needle • scissors (pinking shears optional) • pins
- tape measure or ruler • sewing machine • iron

Confetti Stitched Pillow Covers

I love to blend ordinary décor with a bit of handmade heart to add warmth and hominess to cozy spaces. These fun confetti stitched pillow covers will help you do the same in your own home. Use a variety of simple stitches to make an all-over, one-of-a-kind design—no two will ever be alike!

Supplies:

- solid-colored fabric: 1 square cut to 14″ (35.6cm), 2 pieces cut to 14″ x 10″ (35.6cm x 25.4cm) • a variety of embroidery floss • 6″ or 8″ (15.2cm or 20.3cm) embroidery hoop • embroidery needle • scissors • pins • sewing machine • iron

Instructions for the Embroidered Tote Bag

1 Center a copy of your chosen embroidery design on the front of the tote fabric and transfer the design using carbon tracing paper or a transfer pencil.

2 Place a section of the transferred design into the embroidery hoop. Using a variety of stitches and floss colors, embroider the design. Use back and straight stitches to outline the lines and fill stitches to make solid sections of color. Refer to the stitch section at the front of the book as needed. Finish one section at a time, centering the hoop over each section as you work. Using a variety of different stitches will create depth and texture within the design, and a variety of colors will give the look and style of the Mexican dress.

3 Once you have finished the embroidery, place the embroidered fabric right sides together with the matching piece of fabric. Using ½" (13mm) seam allowance, sew along the sides and bottom of the bag; leave the top unsewn. Repeat to join the two pieces of lining fabric.

4 With the bag and lining pieces still inside out, make a small triangle at the base of each bottom corner by folding the bag so the side seam aligns with the bottom seam. Measure 1½" (3.8cm) up from the corner point, and draw a line across the corner that runs perpendicular to the side seam. Sew along this line, and then trim off the fabric below the stitched line with scissors or pinking shears. Do this to all four corners.

5 Next take the long strap piece, fold the long sides in to the center and iron flat. Fold the strap in half again, matching the long edges, and iron in place. Use a sewing machine to straight stitch down both sides of the strap. Repeat to make the second strap.

6 Turn the main bag section right side out. Leave the lining wrong side out. Tuck the main section into the lining section so that the right sides of both sections are next to each other. Make sure that the seams are centered and that the fabrics are smoothly aligned. Decide where you want to the straps to go, and place a pin where the ends should go (about 3" [7.6cm] from the side seams). Then tuck the strap down in between the main and lining fabrics of the bag front so the raw ends of the strap stick out of the top. Pin the strap and the two layers of fabric in place. Repeat for the other strap on the other side of the bag.

7 Using a sewing machine and a ½" (13mm) seam allowance, straight stitch along the top edge of the bag. Leave a 2" to 3" (5.1cm to 7.6cm) unstitched opening to turn the bag.

8 Pull the tote fabric through the opening and push the lining fabric down inside of the bag. Handstitch the opening closed.

9 Top stitch around the top edge of the bag using a sewing machine, or use a simple embroidery stitch to add a little more embroidered flair. Now you have a useful and pretty tote to take anywhere. I recommend the beach or the market!

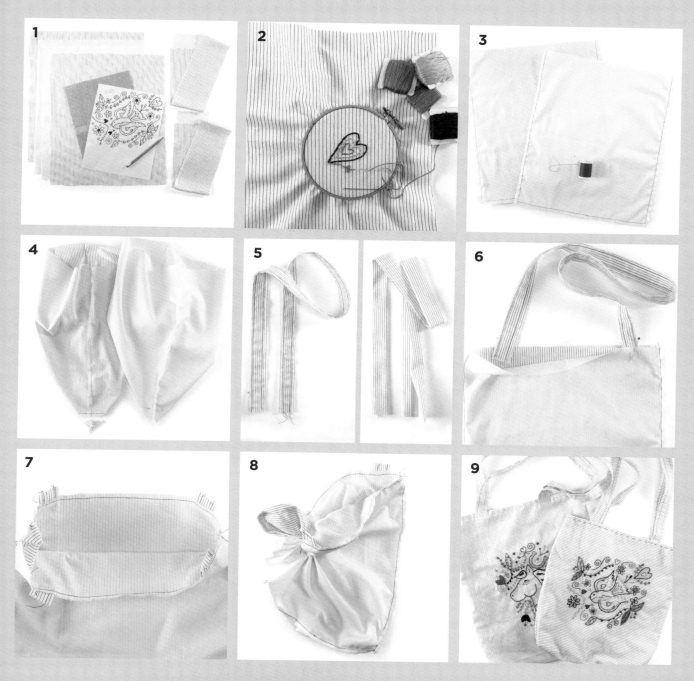

Instructions for the Confetti Stitched Pillow Covers

1 Place the embroidery hoop on one 14" (35.6cm) square of solid-colored fabric where you'd like to start stitching. To make this random pattern, I picked one floss color for each different stitch. Begin using a long piece of one color, and stitch randomly to partially fill the area of the hoop. Then take the next color and add different stitches to the area. Use as many different stitches and colors as you'd like. When you're done filling one area, move the hoop to another. I found it easiest to do the edges first and then work my way toward the middle. Leave unembroidered a little over 1" (2.5cm) margin all the way around the edge so you can later sew the pillow together without sewing over the embroidery.

2 When the embroidery is done, take the two 14" x 10" (35.6cm x 25.4cm) pieces of solid fabric. On each rectangle, press one long edge under about ½" (13mm); fold and press the same edge under again so the raw edge is completely concealed, and then stitch along the folded edge with a sewing machine.

3 Lay the stitched cover face down. On top, place the two backing rectangles face up so the folded edges overlap in the middle. Pin the layers in place around the edge.

4 Use a French seam to complete the pillow cover. Using a sewing machine and a ¼" (6mm) seam allowance, sew all the way around the edge of the pillow cover. Once finished, trim the edges closer to the stitch line, leaving about ⅛" (3mm) seam allowance .

5 Turn the cover inside out and iron the seam so that it is neat and fully pressed out on all edges and corners. Using a sewing machine and a ¼" (6mm) seam allowance, sew all the way around the edge again. This will create a finished, enclosed French seam.

6 Turn the cover right side out and iron the edge once more. Insert a 12" (30.5cm) pillow form and you're finished.

Geometric Necklace

Inspired by the clean lines of modern art and the simplicity of Navajo folk pieces, this hand-stitched necklace is sure to make a statement. Using quick embroidery stitches and a few materials, this bold necklace is perfect for dressing up a plain dress or T-shirt.

Supplies:

• templates (page 133) • cardboard or cardstock • 2 colors of felt sheets
• 2 small pieces of complementary patterned fabric • 3 colors of embroidery floss
• (2) 12" (30.5cm) pieces of satiny ribbon in a coordinating color • (6) $\frac{1}{4}$" (6mm) jump rings • embroidery needle • scissors • pins • tape measure or ruler

Denim Doodle Skirt

Be a trendsetter with your very own denim doodle skirt! This hip, one-of-a-kind skirt is sure to make you the envy of all your friends. With a classic A-line cut, it's as flattering as it is fun. Choose your favorite doodle to make an all-over print, or use several for a sketchbook look.

Supplies:

• embroidery designs (page 135) • carbon tracing paper or transfer pencil
• at least 1 yard (1 meter) of thick cotton fabric or denim • $\frac{1}{4}$" to $\frac{1}{2}$" (6mm to 13mm) wide elastic • a variety of embroidery floss • embroidery hoop • embroidery needle
• scissors and pinking shears • pins • chalk pencil • tape measure or ruler
• sewing machine • iron

Instructions for the Geometric Necklace

1 Photocopy, enlarge and cut out all of the templates from heavy paper. Using the large shape templates, cut two felt trapezoids, two felt triangles, four felt squares and four felt circles. (Each shape will have two layers of felt for extra sturdiness.) Cut the fabric appliqués from the smaller templates, one for each shape, matching the fabric to the felt shapes as desired. Center and pin a fabric appliqué to one of each felt shape, and then appliqué stitch all the way around the fabric shape. Try to space the stitches so that any pointed edges are covered by a stitch; this also helps the edges from fraying.

2 For the necklace chain, cut two pieces of ribbon about 12" (30.5cm) long (or any length depending on how you'd like to wear the necklace). Place the remaining felt shape on the back of the appliquéd felt shape. Starting with the outside squares, place about ½" (13mm) of the ribbon in between the layers of felt at one of the points, and straight stitch through both layers just outside the fabric appliqué. When you come to the ribbon, double the stitch for extra strength. When finished, knot and tie the thread on the back of the shape. Repeat this step for the other outside square.

3 Complete the rest of the shapes in the same way, straight stitching through both layers of felt, and knot and tie on the back of each shape to finish. Now it's time for the jump rings that will bring the piece together. If you are re-creating my project here, simply place the jump rings where shown. If you are creating your own unique necklace, lay out all the shapes so the edges touch to judge where they will connect to each other best. Use the embroidery needle to make a little hole through both layers of felt where the jump ring will go (not too close to any edge). This will make it easier to slip the jump rings through. Do this for all pieces that need a jump ring. Then slip the jump rings through the holes in each piece, connecting the shapes as desired, and close the rings.

4 Tie a bow with the ribbons to finish.

Get Creative
Feel free to use as many shapes as you'd like to make your own unique statement piece. For smaller shapes, try backing the fabric with fusible interfacing to make the fabric a little thicker, stiffer and easier to cut.

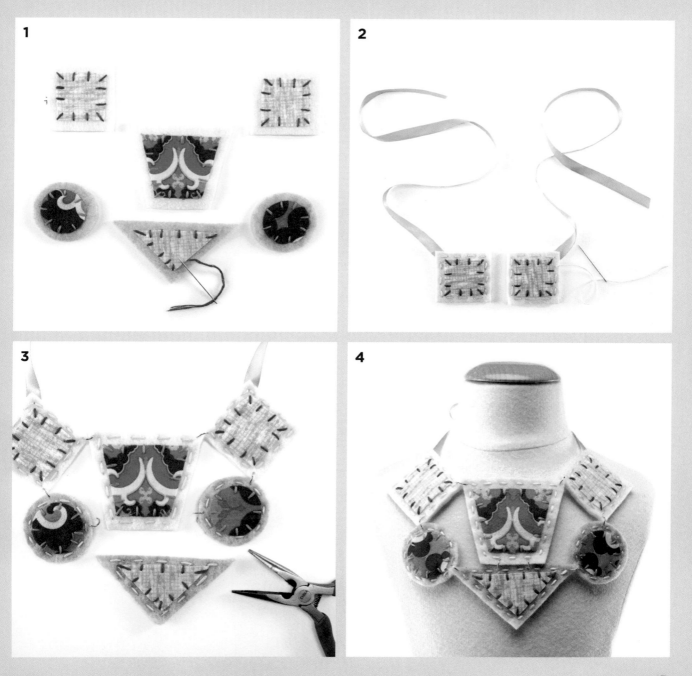

Instructions for the Denim Doodle Skirt

1 Measure your waist—your natural waist at the thinnest part, or 2" to 3" (5.1cm to 7.6cm) below it, if you like your skirts to sit lower—and your hips, at the widest part of your thighs and rear. To determine how wide you'd like the skirt to be at the bottom, wrap a tape measure around your knees and then open your stance to the width you want the skirt bottom; note this measurement. Determine the length you want for your skirt by measuring down from your waist. Add about 2" to 3" (5.1cm to 7.6cm) to your waist measurement, and add 4" to 6" (10.2cm to 15.2cm) to your hip measurement. Add another 1" (2.5cm) to all measurements to allow room for seams.

Fold the yardage of cotton/denim lengthwise in half; then fold in half again so you have four stacked layers with one center fold and the four raw edges aligned. Halve each of the measurements you determined earlier. Measuring from the fold outward, mark each of your measurement points with chalk pencil: one for your waist, one for your hips, and one for the bottom width at the desired length. Cut the skirt at a diagonal through each of the points and straight across the top and bottom. This makes two identical skirt pieces.

2 While the fabric is still folded, starting at the bottom edge of the skirt, cut the outside point so it is rounded slightly upward. This prevents the sides of the skirt from hanging down lower than the rest of the skirt. Repeat for the other side of the skirt.

3 Now we're ready to sew! Place and pin both sides of the skirt wrong sides together. Using a sewing machine, sew a ½" (13mm) wide seam down both sides of the skirt. Then trim the edges about ¼" (6mm) outside of the stitch line.

4 Turn the skirt inside out and iron the seams. Then sew another ½" (13mm) wide seam down both edges, creating an enclosed seam along both sides of the skirt. Turn the skirt right side out and iron the seams to one side.

5 Fold and press the bottom edge of the skirt under to the wrong side. Sew completely around the bottom. Trim the raw edge of the hem with pinking shears to create a neat edge.

6 To make the waistband, fold the top edge under to the wrong side by about ¼" (6mm). Fold the same edge under again to completely conceal the raw edge. Then fold under a third time about 1" (2.5cm) to make another seam. Begin sewing about 1" (2.5cm) down on the top of the skirt and through the first folded edge that you created. Leave a few inches (approximately 10cm) unsewn when you are almost finished to insert the elastic. Cut the elastic to your waist measurement and place a safety pin at one end. Holding on to one end of the elastic so it doesn't get pulled into the hole, guide the safety pin through the waistband until you reach the other side. Machine or hand sew both sides of the elastic together, then sew the hold in the waist band closed.

7 Using carbon tracing paper or transfer pencil, transfer your chosen embroidery designs to the skirt. I started at the bottom and worked my way up to the top randomly. Working one at a time, place the embroidery hoop around each transferred design and begin stitching, using whatever colors and designs you like.

8 Wear with your favorite blouse and get ready for constant compliments!

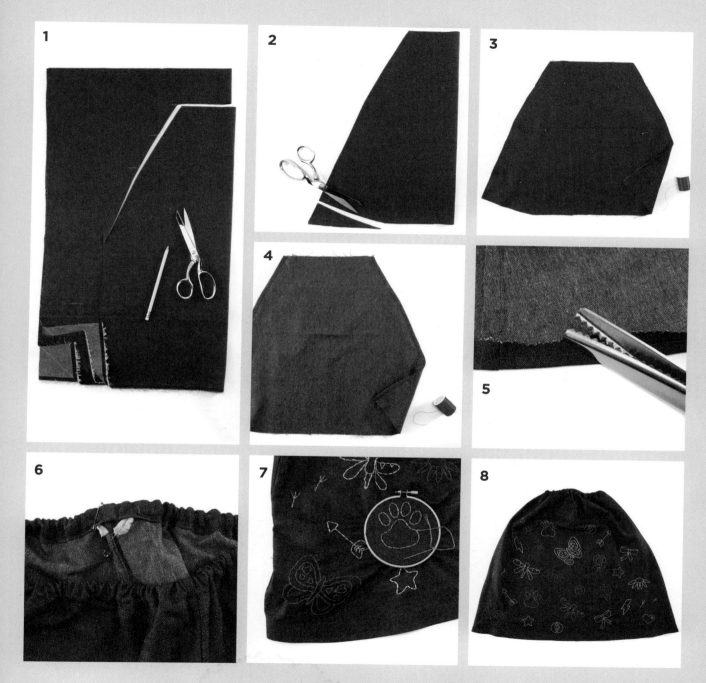

Mini Softie Pins and Keychains

Lions, pandas and ladybugs, oh my! These wildlife-inspired cuties are great for animal or nature lovers. Turn them into pins that can be worn and paired together, keychains to give as fun little trinkets, or simply handmade keepsakes or toys.

Supplies:

• templates (page 133) • cardboard or cardstock • felt (3 shades of brown for the lion; green for the leaf; black, white and dark gray for the panda; black and red for the ladybug) • floss (3 shades of brown to match lion felt; 1 contrasting green for the leaf; black, white, gray and an eye color for the panda; black and an eye color for the ladybug) • ribbon • stuffing • key rings • pinbacks • embroidery needle • scissors and pinking shears • pins • tape measure or ruler

Instructions for the Mini Softie Pins and Keychains

1 Photocopy, enlarge and cut out all of the templates from heavy paper. Cut all of the appropriate colors for each of the templates and two pieces each for the main template for the back side of the softies. Use the photos as a guide for the felt colors as you cut each piece.

Note: If you are making the Panda or Lion, freehand cut a small triangle for the nose.

2 Using simple straight stitches, layer and appliqué all of the felt shapes to the front piece of the mini softie. Use small star stitches on the back of the ladybug for dots and tiny layered straight stitches to create eyes on the creatures. For the leaf, straight stitch down the center and off to each side to make veins.

3 When you have completed the front side of each mini softie, decide whether you'd like them to become pins or keychains.

For keychains, cut a 3" (7.6cm) piece of ribbon and slip it through the center of the key ring. Layer the softie pieces and pin them in place. Slip the ribbon ends in between the front and back layers of felt, forming as big a loop as you'd like. Straight stitch around the outside edge. When you come to the ribbon, double stitch to secure the ribbon in place. Toward the end, leave about 1" (2.5cm) open and lightly stuff the softie for shape. Once stuffed, complete the straight stitch and knot and tie on the back to finish.

For softie pins, place the pinback in the middle of the backing felt piece and stitch the pinback in place. (I like to use pinbacks that have a flat bottom with holes so that they are easily stitched on.) Cut a small rectangle of matching felt to hide the bottom of the pinback and use an appliqué stitch around the edges to secure the square. Then, with wrong sides together and edges lined up, straight stitch along the edge of the creature, leaving about 1" (2.5cm) open to lightly stuff for shape. Once stuffed, complete the straight stitch and knot and tie on the back to finish.

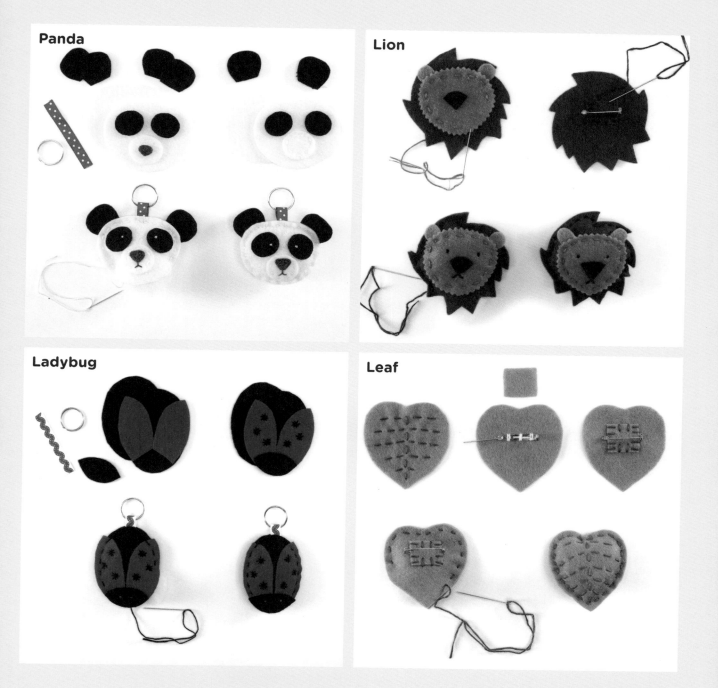

Panda

Lion

Ladybug

Leaf

53

Tulip Placemats With Leaf Table Runner

A perfect addition to your next garden party or spring holiday spread, this cute set of tulip placemats and leaf table runner is a bold and colorful way to make your table fancy. Created with an easy straight stitch and a variety of pretty felts, these pieces are guaranteed to spruce up your table and make it festive for your next springtime gathering. Add a bouquet of beautiful fresh-cut flowers for a simple yet stunning display.

Supplies:

• templates (page 136) • cardboard or cardstock • ½ yard (0.5m) each of 2 shades of green felt • 3 sheets of felt in a variety of colors for each flower • 1 fat quarter of felt in your main flower color for each as your backing • embroidery floss (2 shades of green; 1 color for each flower) • embroidery needle • scissors • pins • tape measure or ruler

Instructions for the Tulip Placemats With Leaf Table Runner

For the tulip placemats:

1 Photocopy, enlarge and cut out all of the flower templates from heavy paper. For each flower, cut one felt flower center, two felt outside petals (left and right), and two felt inside petals. Make the flower center the main color and use two other colors to boldly accent the flower, or use the same color felt for all petals.

To begin constructing the flowers, pin the two outside petals on top of the flower center, lining it up the bottom and center edges. Pin the two inside petals behind the center so they pop up in the middle of the two points. Straight stitch along all of the inside seams in each place the flowers come together. Leave the very top and outsides of the petals unstitched.

2 The petals now form one piece. Lay the entire flower on top of the fat quarter or larger piece of felt and pin in place. Using the flower you've just made as the template, cut along the entire outside edge so you have a full flower shape to use as the backing.

3 Keeping the top pinned to the backing, straight stitch all the way around the outer edges and top of the flower, sewing about $\frac{1}{4}''$ (6mm) from the edge. Knot and tie off in the back to finish.

4 Repeat the previous steps to make the desired number of placemats.

For the leaf table runner:

5 Photocopy, enlarge and cut out the leaf template from heavy paper. Cut eight leaves from each of the two different colors of green felt. Take four leaves of each green (eight total) and, using two different colors of embroidery floss (one for each color of felt), straight stitch down the center of each leaf. Pin the remaining leaf shapes to the backs of the leaves to become the backing.

6 Using the same floss color that you stitched down the center of the leaf with, straight stitch each layered leaf all the way around the edge so the front and back are stitched together.

7 When you are finished stitching all of the leaf fronts and backs together, lay them out so that they are staggered back and forth and so each leaf meets up with another at one point. Where each of the leaves touch, sew a large cross stitch to connect the two leaves. Alternate greens and cross stitch colors for the best look.

8 Continue until all of the leaves are sewn together in a long row.

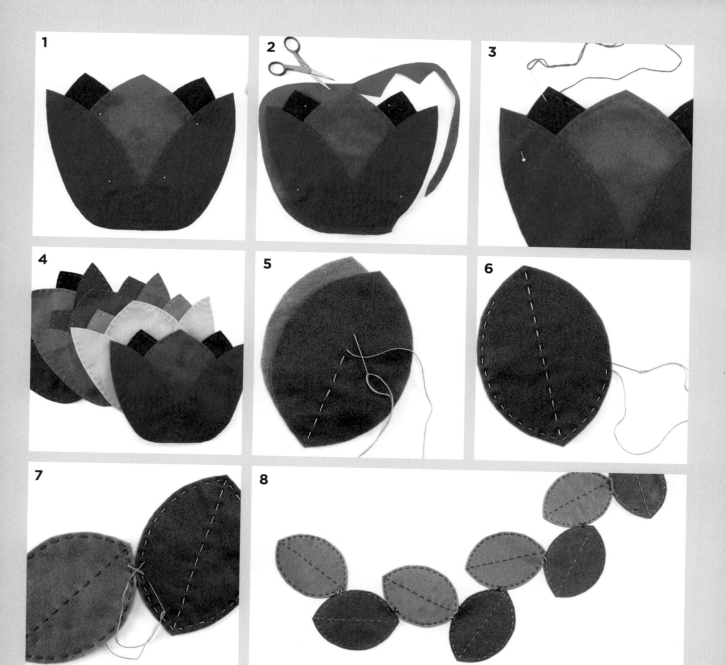

Cookout Kitchen Wall Hanging

What some folks call junk food, I call comfort food. A yummy hot dog, soda and fries remind me of summer cookouts, the Fourth of July and a simple home-cooked meal. Reminiscent of the wonderful graphic qualities of vintage signage, this fun, plush wall hanging for your kitchen is sure to bring smiles and reminders of summer fun.

Supplies:

• templates (page 137) • cardboard or cardstock • 7 colors of felt (tan and red for the hot dog; yellow, white and an accent color for the fries; white, brown and an accent color for the soda) • coordinating embroidery floss for each felt color • yellow rickrack • ribbon • stuffing • embroidery needle • scissors and pinking shears • pins

Vintage-Style Half Apron

In this patchwork project, we'll create a half apron with true vintage style that will make you want to head to the kitchen and get cookin'! Created from felt and a variety of patterned fabrics, you'll look lovely while baking your next batch of chocolate chip cookies or entertaining at your next cookout. The look is complete with a big felt strawberry appliqué that becomes the pocket.

Supplies:

• templates (page 136) • cardboard or cardstock • 4 different patterned fabrics • 4 felt sheets (2 in red or pink for the strawberry appliqué, 1 in green for the top, 1 in another color for seeds) • 3 colors of embroidery floss matching each of your felt strawberry pieces • embroidery needle • scissors and pinking shears • pins • tape measure or ruler • sewing machine • iron

Instructions for the Cookout Kitchen Wall Hanging

1 Photocopy, enlarge and cut out all of the templates from heavy paper. From felt, cut two tan completed hot dog shapes, two white fry container backs, and two white soda bottles. Cut a third soda bottle from brown felt and cut off the top of the bottle (refer to photos). Freehand cut several yellow felt French fries with pinking shears, making the fries varied lengths and widths. From contrasting felt, freehand cut accent shapes the width of the fry container and a label for the soda bottle the width of the bottle. Cut one red felt hot dog, one tan small bun and one tan large bun.

2 Place the small bun and the hot dog on top of a completed hog dog shape. Straight stitch along the top edge of the hot dog only. Layer the large bun so that it overlaps the bottom of the hot dog, and stitch along the top edge only. Cut a piece of yellow rickrack for mustard and straight stitch it to the hot dog. Next, straight stitch the accent shapes onto the fry container front. Form each fry from two layers of felt for more fullness, and straight stitch the layers together. Lay the finished fries on top of the fry container back and place the container front on top, lining up all edges. Straight stitch across the container front to hold the fries in place. Finally, layer one white soda bottle, the brown soda bottle and the accent label. Straight stitch along the top of the brown and along the top and bottom of the soda label.

3 Pin the completed fry front section to the remaining fry container back. Cut a long piece of ribbon and tie a knot at one end. Sandwich the knot at the top center of the container in between the felt layers. Straight stitch around the fry container, doubling the stitch when you reach the ribbon and leaving an opening for stuffing. Stuff the fry container for shape and then stitch the opening closed. Knot and tie on the back when finished. Layer, stitch and stuff the soda bottle in the same way, knotting and tying the thread on the back each time you begin a new color.

Pin the hot dog section to the completed hot dog back. Cut a long piece of ribbon for the top of the hot dog and tie knots at each end. Sandwich both ends along the top edge of the hot dog in between the felt layers. Stitch the layers together along the top edge of the hot dog only, using floss to match each of the shapes. Double the straight stitches when you come to the ribbon. Knot and tie on the back when finished. Sew a few straight stitches in red floss through both layers of felt at each hot dog end.

4 Tie a knot at the top of the fry and soda ribbons, and place each between the two layers of felt at either end of the hot dog, far enough apart so that they won't touch when hanging. Straight stitch along the bottom of the hot dog, double stitching through the ribbons. Leave a small space open to insert stuffing. Stuff the hot dog fully and then stitch the opening closed. Knot and tie on the back when finished.

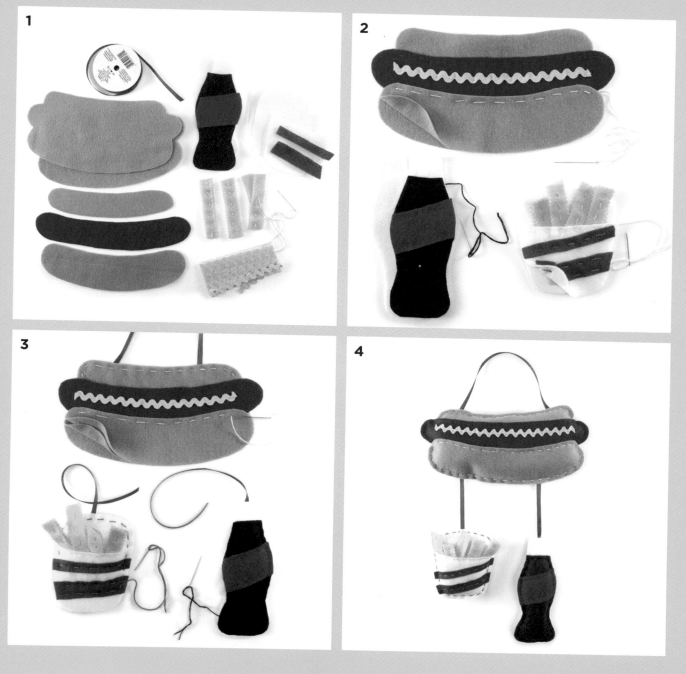

Instructions for the Vintage-Style Half Apron

1 From each of two patterned fabrics, cut three 7½" x 5½" (19.1cm x 14cm) rectangles. These will become the patchwork on the front of the apron. From a third patterned fabric, cut two 4" x 14½" (10.2cm x 36.8cm) rectangles for the side panels and two 3" x 30" (7.6cm x 76.2cm) rectangles for the belt. From a fourth patterned fabric, cut one 4" x 30" (10.2cm x 76.2cm) rectangle for the waistband and one 22½" x 14½" (57.2cm x 36.8cm) rectangle for the back lining.

Arrange the six 7½" x 5½" (19.1cm x 14cm) rectangles so that they are alternating in two rows of three. Using ¼" seam allowance and a sewing machine, sew the rectangles together to form rows, and then sew the two rows together. (If you need to make the apron larger, just cut and add a few more columns to the patchwork.) Now sew the 4" x 14½" (10.2cm x 36.8cm) side panels to either side of the patchworked rectangles.

2 Photocopy, enlarge and cut out all of the strawberry templates from heavy paper. Cut two strawberries from pink or red felt and two leafy tops from green felt. From the third felt color, cut as many seed shapes as you want.

3 Layer the two strawberry shapes, sandwich them between the two leafy top shapes and pin all four layers in place. Randomly pin the seed pieces on top of the strawberry. Stitch the seeds in place using matching embroidery floss. With the green or yellow embroidery floss, straight stitch around the entire leaf shape to stitch all four layers of the strawberry together.

1

4 Place the strawberry on top of the patchwork, positioning it where you'd like. Straight stitch along the red strawberry with a floss color of your choice to secure it on the patchwork. Don't stitch along the leafy top; this leaves an opening for the pocket.

5 Place and pin the 22½" x 14½" (57.2cm x 36.8cm) lining fabric right sides together with the apron front. Using ½" seam allowance and a sewing machine, sew along both sides and the bottom edge; don't sew across the top edge of the apron. Then sew a diagonal line across both bottom corners, about 2" (5.1cm) in on the diagonal, to create a faux rounded edge. Cut off the corners, leaving about ½" (13mm) of fabric outside of the sewn diagonal line. Turn the apron right side out. (continued on page 64)

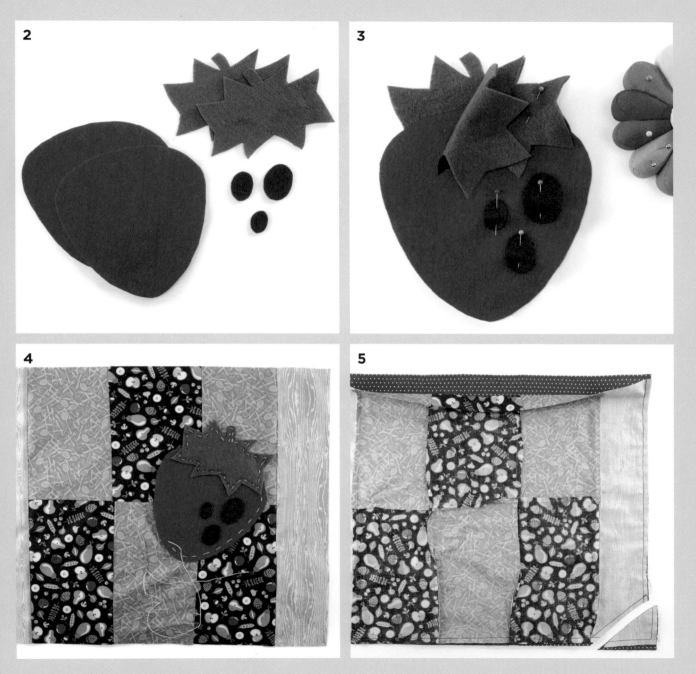

6 Fold and press both 3" x 30" (7.6cm x 76.2cm) belt rectangles in half lengthwise. Use your sewing machine to sew down the length of each folded strip, staying close to the raw edges. Use pinking shears to cut along the raw edges, just outside of the stitches, to create a fun jagged edge that will prevent fraying.

7 Fold and press the waistband rectangle in half lengthwise to create a crease. Open the crease. Fold and press the long edges under about 1" (2.5cm). Fold and press both short ends under a little less than a 1/2" (13mm); fold and press under again to completely conceal the raw edges.

8 Place the apron top along the fold on the waistband, lining it up so that the apron is centered on the band.

9 Place a belt in between the layered waistband on each side of the apron and pin the pieces together. Top stitch all the way across the bottom edge of the waistband to sew the waistband to the apron. Use a needle and embroidery floss to sew cross stitches along the end of the waistband where it meets the belt; this secures the belt to the waistband. Knot and tie when finished.

10 To conceal the raw belt ends, freehand cut four large felt circles. Sandwich a belt end between two circles and straight stitch around the circles. Repeat this step for the other end as well.

11 The apron is complete and you're ready to get cookin'!

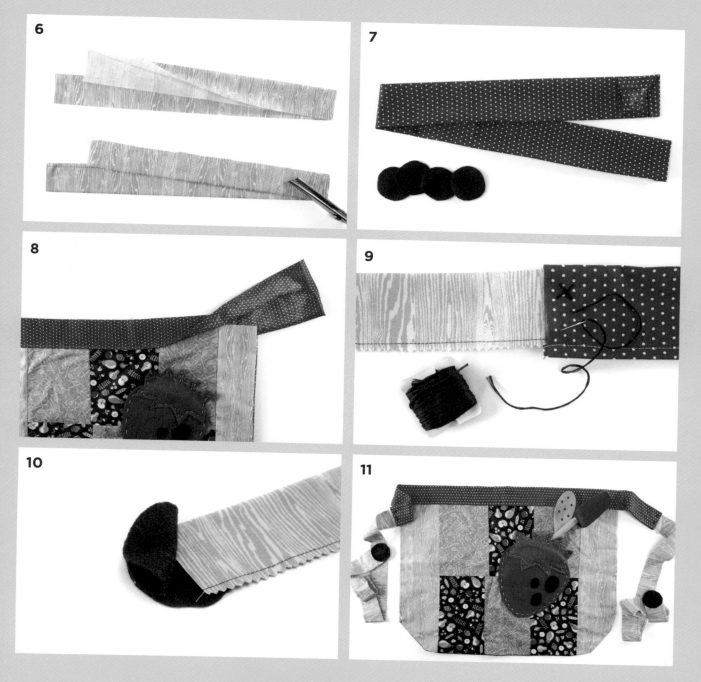

Modern Penny Rugs

Penny rugs are rooted in old-time folk art traditions. They've been around since the 1800s and are as useful as they are pretty. Often made into full rugs, pillows, wall hangings or table toppers, they allowed folks to use small pieces of leftover materials to make a unique, decorative fiber art piece. The most common penny rug motif features layered circles appliquéd in place. We'll make a trio of penny rugs with a modern twist, stitching up a pretty butterfly, a happy flower and a classic geometric design using felt, fabric, embroidery and variegated floss.

Supplies for Geometric Penny Rug:

• templates (page 137) • cardboard or cardstock • 2 felt sheets for the base, 5 colors of felt for the appliqués • 1 color of variegated embroidery floss • embroidery needle • scissors • pins

Supplies for Butterfly Penny Rug:

• templates (page 137) • cardboard or cardstock • 2 felt sheets for the base, 5 colors of felt for the appliqués • 1 small piece of patterned fabric • scissors • 1 color of variegated embroidery floss • embroidery needle • scissors • pins

Supplies for Happy Face Flower Penny Rug:

• templates (page 137) • cardboard or cardstock • 2 felt sheets for the base, 5 colors of felt for the petals, 2 colors for the eyes, 1 for the mouth • 1 piece of patterned fabric (about a fat quarter or less) for the petals • 2 colors of variegated embroidery floss • 3 colors of embroidery floss to match the 2 eye colors and mouth color • embroidery needle • scissors • pins

Instructions for the Geometric Penny Rug

1 Photocopy, enlarge and cut out all of the templates from heavy paper. Cut two felt arrows from two different colors, two felt diamonds from a third color, two felt stars from a fourth color and one felt oval from a fifth color. Cut two large squares out of the base felt using the template.

Line up all of the shapes on one base square so they are evenly spaced and slightly away from the edges. Pin all of the pieces in place. Appliqué stitch around the edges of the appliqué shapes until they are all securely in place. Use cross stitches and star stitches anywhere you like to add a little interest.

2 Pin the remaining base square on the back of the penny rug. Blanket stitch around all four edges to sew the back and front together. To finish the blanket stitch, loop through the first stitch and then through the layers of felt, pulling the thread through the back of the piece.

3 Knot and tie when finished. For a variation, try using the same shapes to make a different pattern or a different floss color on every shape. Using the variegated floss gives the illusion of using different floss colors.

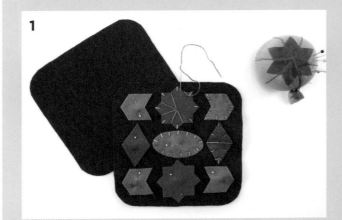

Instructions for the Butterfly Penny Rug

1 Photocopy, enlarge and cut out all of the templates from heavy paper. Cut two butterfly shapes out of the same color of felt. Cut two of wing shapes 1, 2 and 3, each shape out of a different shade of felt. Cut one wing shape 4 out of a pretty patterned fabric. Then flip the wing 4 template over and cut a second fabric shape. Using the diamond template, cut three diamonds of one felt color and two of another felt color. We'll use one shade of variegated floss for the whole design.

Evenly place the three matching diamonds vertically on one felt butterfly shape: one at the top, one at the bottom and one in the middle. Use a star stitch and variegated floss to secure each in place. Now place the remaining two felt diamonds in the spaces in between, slightly overlapping the existing diamonds. Use a star stitch to secure them in place. Pin the wing shapes onto the butterfly as shown. Appliqué or straight stitch around all of the shapes, and knot and tie the thread on the back when finished.

2 Pin the remaining butterfly shape on the back of the penny rug. Blanket stitch around the outside edge to sew the back and front together. To finish the blanket stitch, loop through the first stitch and then through the layers of felt, pulling the thread through the back of the piece.

3 Knot and tie on the back side when you are finished.

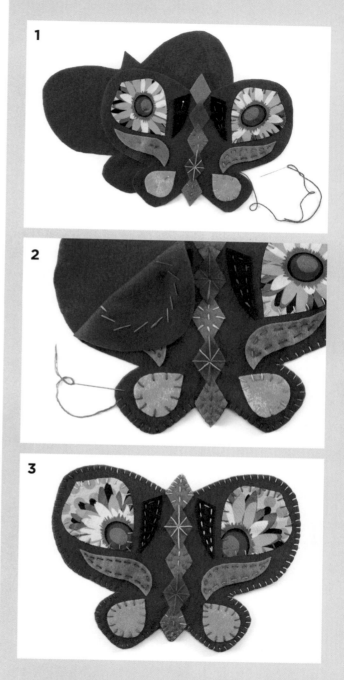

69

Instructions for the Happy Flower Penny Rug

1 Photocopy, enlarge and cut out all of the templates from heavy paper. Cut two felt face circles. Next, cut two large felt ovals for the outside eye and two small felt ovals for the inner eye. Cut one mouth from another color of felt. Cut twenty large outer petals total—four each of five different colors of felt. Using the inner petal template, cut ten pieces of patterned fabric (or felt) to accent your petals.

2 Center, pin and appliqué stitch each fabric inner petal to one half of each felt outer petal. Use one color of variegated floss to appliqué the petal shapes.

3 Once you have finished appliquéing all of the petals, pin the remaining felt pieces of the same color on the back sides. Straight stitch along the edge to join the front and back of the petal, using a different shade of variegated floss. Knot and tie on the back when finished.

4 Pin the large eye ovals to one face circle and straight stitch all the way around the edges. Next place the smaller eye ovals where you'd like and straight stitch with matching floss. Straight stitch the mouth in place using matching floss.

5 Lay out the remaining large felt circle and place all of the petals around the outside edge, alternating petal colors. Place the face piece on top and make sure the bottom edges of the petals are not showing. Pin the petals in place. Straight stitch along the edge of the happy face circle through all the layers, using the same variegated floss used to straight stitch the petals.

6 Knot and tie on the back when finished.

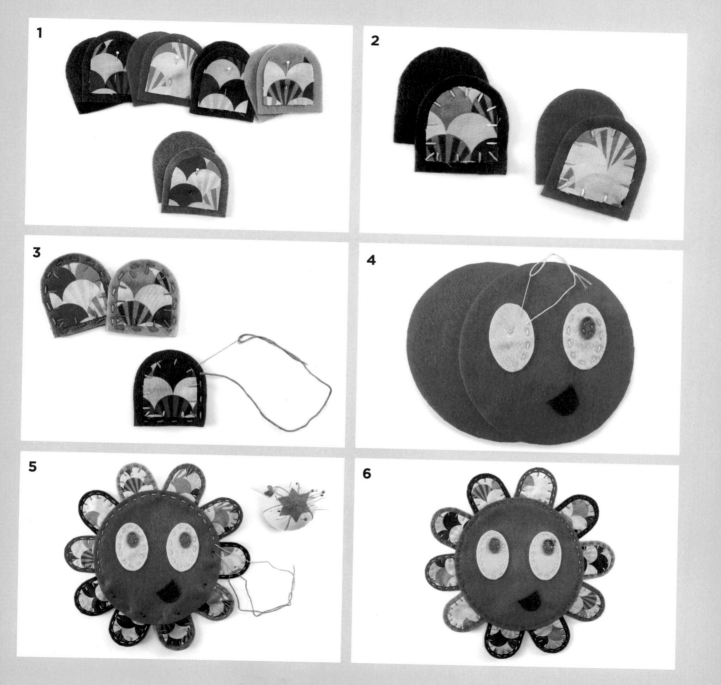

Postcard Mail Sorter

A postcard mail sorter is a great way to organize your real-life inbox! In this project, create a unique mail sorter that is shaped like a giant postcard using felt and embroidery techniques. Send and receive love notes from your sweetie, or just keep all your important mail in one place. Use it to store all your lovely scraps such as postcards from a friend, pen pal mail, kids' drawings or your favorite doodles.

Supplies:

• templates (page 138) • 3 pieces of felt or stiffened felt: 2 cut to 15½" x 11" (39.4cm x 27.9cm), 1 cut to 15½" x 6" (39.4cm x 15.2cm) • 5 colors of felt for the appliqués • a variety of embroidery floss to accent the designs • ribbon • stuffing • embroidery needle • scissors and pinking shears • pins • tape measure or ruler

Fabric and Yarn Lamp Shade

Make those accent lamps really pop by mixing patterns and colors to create a unique lamp shade to go with your décor. It's always difficult to find the perfect matching shade, so why not make your own by pairing pretty patterned fabrics and festive yarn? These one-of-a-kind shades will add a bit of charm that you just can't find at the store.

Supplies:

• flat paper lamp shade in desired size • several different scraps of patterned fabric, or 3 to 4 fat quarters • wax paper • coordinating yarn • clear fabric glue • paint/foam brush • scissors

Instructions for the Postcard Mail Sorter

1 Photocopy, enlarge and cut out all of the templates from heavy paper. Cut the shapes out of the desired colors of felt. Cut the two stamp rectangles from two different colors of felt using pinking shears. Cut three squiggles for the postmark. Cut two pieces of ribbon about 3" (7.6cm) long. Cut two 1" (2.5cm) squares from scrap felt.

2 On the 15½" x 6" (39.4cm x 15.2cm) rectangle, straight stitch several "writing" lines on the right side only. Straight stitch the fleur-de-lis felt shape anywhere on the left. Straight stitch about ¼" (6mm) from the top all the way across the top of the rectangle.

3 Place the rectangle you just stitched on top of one 15½" x 11" (39.2cm x 27.9cm) rectangle. Line up the bottom edges and pin in place. Beginning at the bottom middle, straight stitch a vertical straight line all the way to the top of the large rectangle.

4 For the felt stamp, center and pin the small stamp rectangle on top of the large stamp rectangle. Place the stamp in the upper right corner of the postcard, leaving enough room to stitch around the edge later. Secure the stamp in place using a variety of stitches (straight stitch, cross stitch and V stitch). Freehand stitch a cent symbol or a value for the stamp on the small rectangle. (I used a back stitch.) For the postmark, center and pin the heart on the circle. Straight stitch all the way around the edge of the heart, lightly stuffing the heart as you near the end. Place and pin the postmark squiggles slightly over the stamp, and straight stitch in place. Pin the postmark circle over the ends of the squiggles and straight stitch around the edge to finish. Add a few more straight stitches in the upper left corner for the return address.

5 On the remaining large rectangle piece, evenly place the two scrap squares on each side near the top. Loop the ribbons and tuck the raw ends under the squares. Straight stitch each small square to the back of the postcard, doubling the stitches when you come to the ribbons to secure.

6 With wrong sides together and edges matched and pinned, straight stitch the large squares together, sewing about ¼" (6mm) in along all four edges of the postcard.

7 Knot and tie on the back when finished, and hang your new mail sorter from the ribbons on the back.

Personalize It!
To personalize the postcard even more, you could compose a sweet message or put a name on the writing lines using stitched handwriting (flip back to page 12 to learn how).

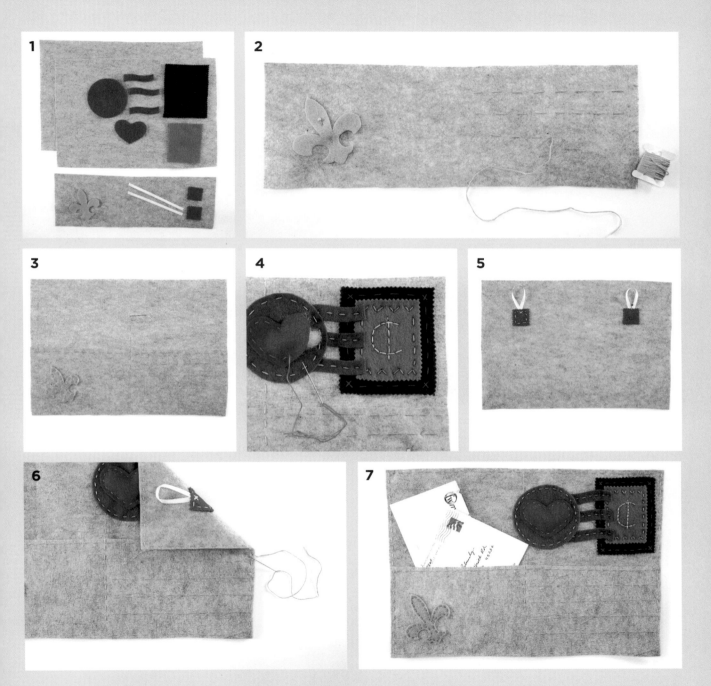

Instructions for the Fabric and Yarn Lamp Shade

1 Place the paper lamp shade on wax paper. Cut the fabric into small squares and different random shapes. Use a brush to apply glue directly onto the shade, spreading on enough glue for the size of the piece of fabric you wish to adhere. Next, place the piece of fabric onto the glue and press in place. Brush a bit more glue over the edges and top of the fabric if necessary.

1

2 Apply fabric all the way around the shade instead of working in one small area first. This will help to spread out the different patterns and make the design more even. Work as closely to the edge of the shade as you can but fill the entire space of the shade first before tackling the edges.

3 When finished, cut a few more pieces to go around the top and bottom edge of the shade. Make sure to place glue in the inside edges as well so the fabric will wrap around the bottom of the shade. Once you've completed the shade, let it dry overnight in a cool, dry place.

4 Once the shade is completely dry, add the yarn accents. Cut several long pieces of yarn. Starting with one cut end on the inside of the lamp, wrap the yarn around the shade from top to bottom in the same place several times until you create the desired look.

5 When finished, knot and tie the tails together on the inside of the lamp. Repeat as many times as you'd like, going around the entire shade.

6 Pair with your favorite lamp base and enjoy!

Bunting-Style Window Valance

Delightful and spunky, this unique valance is sure to spruce up any room. It's perfect for letting some light into your space, and it looks great on windows of all sizes. You'll be able to whip up this fun valance in an afternoon using simple hand- and machine-sewing techniques and playful notions!

Supplies:

• 1 yard (1m) of patterned fabric • 1 yard (1m) of solid colored fabric • ½ yard (0.5m) of 72" (182.9cm) felt • variety of buttons (1½" [3.8cm] or larger) • embroidery floss • scissors • embroidery needle • sewing machine

Instructions for the Bunting-Style Window Valance

1 Measure and cut 20" x 5" (50.8cm x 12.7cm) rectangles of patterned fabric; cut as many as you need to cover the width of your window (leaving a small space between rectangles). Cut the same number of 20" x 5" (50.8cm x 12.7cm) rectangles from the solid lining fabric. Next, cut a rectangle from the long piece of felt that measures approximately 6" (15.2cm) wide by the width of your window. Add more width to the felt if you need it for a large circular curtain rod.

2 Place a patterned fabric rectangle right sides together with a solid fabric rectangle. Using ½" (13mm) seam allowance and a sewing machine, sew the rectangles together along both long sides and one short side (the bottom); leave the top open. Repeat this with all of the fabric rectangles. Turn the sewn rectangles right side out and press them with an iron.

3 Fold and finger press the felt rectangle in half lengthwise. Tuck the top/open end of the fabric rectangles into the folded felt piece, spacing the rectangles evenly across the felt piece.

4 Using an embroidery needle and floss, sew a row of cross stitches along the bottom edge of the folded piece of felt; leave the sides open to create a pocket for the curtain rod. Or, pin the rectangles in place and sewing along the seam with a sewing machine.

5 Now sew big buttons to the bottom of each of the rectangles with colorful embroidery floss.

6 Use a standard curtain rod to hang your fabulous curtains in the window.

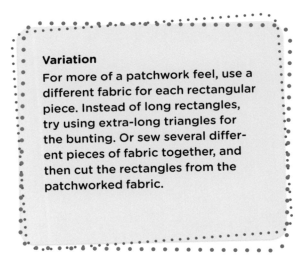

Variation
For more of a patchwork feel, use a different fabric for each rectangular piece. Instead of long rectangles, try using extra-long triangles for the bunting. Or sew several different pieces of fabric together, and then cut the rectangles from the patchworked fabric.

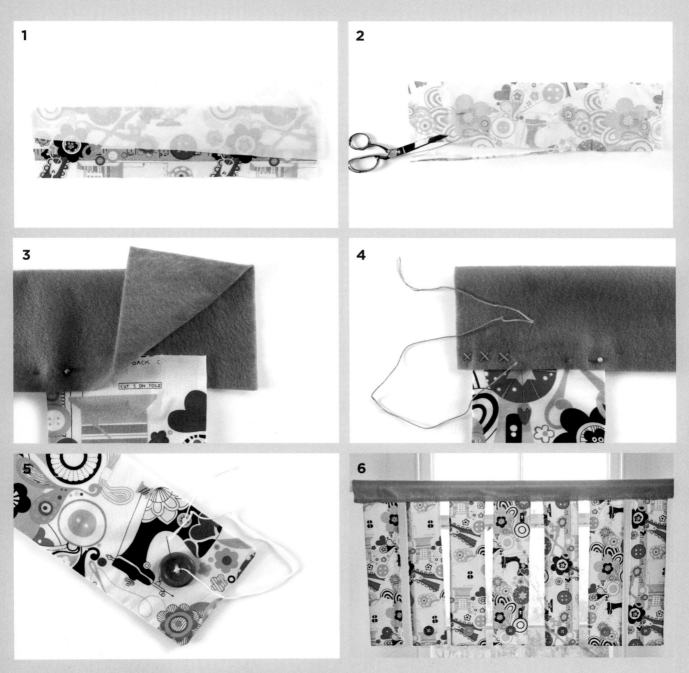

Felt and Ribbon Bookmarks

Don't dog-ear those pages! Dress up your latest read with a fancy bookmark instead. Hold your pages with three different designs—classic, heart-shaped or circle style—that use small pieces of fabric and quick stitches. These make perfect gifts for the bookworms in your life.

Supplies:

• templates (page 138) • cardboard or cardstock • a variety of colors of felt
• small pieces of patterned fabric • coordinating embroidery floss in several colors • ribbon or rickrack • buttons • other embellishments as desired
• embroidery needle • scissors • pins • tape measure

Embroidery Hoop Mobile

Add a bit of movement and visual interest to your décor with an eye-catching embroidery hoop mobile. By using a variety of fabrics and trims, such as lace and ribbon, you'll create unique hoops that will spin, twirl and let the sunshine through. Contrasting fabrics will bring a splash of color to your space.

Supplies:

• embroidery hoops: 1 large (7" [17.8cm] or bigger) and several smaller ones in a variety of sizes
• 2 patterned fabrics large enough to place in your hoops • ribbon • lace • stuffing
• 2 colors of embroidery floss (1 neutral for the hanging threads, 1 to embellish)
• quick-drying craft glue, for securing hoops • embroidery needle • scissors • pins

Instructions for the Classic Bookmark

1 Photocopy, enlarge and cut out all of the templates from heavy paper. Cut two large rectangles out of felt and one small rectangle out of fabric.

2 Center and pin the fabric rectangle on top of one felt rectangle. Appliqué stitch all the way around the edge of the fabric. When you are finished, embellish the fabric with a few extra top stitches or a few buttons. (I used cross stitches to embellish mine.)

3 Layer the sewn top with the remaining felt rectangle. Cut a few pieces of ribbon in varied lengths, loop them in half and sandwich the raw edges between the two pieces of felt. Work a straight stitch all the way around to complete the bookmark.

Classic Bookmark

Instructions for the Circle Bookmark

1 Photocopy, enlarge and cut out all of the circle templates from heavy paper. For the bookmark top, cut one large and one medium felt circles, and one large and one small fabric circles. For the bookmark bottom, cut two more medium felt circles and one small fabric circle. Cut one piece of ribbon to the desired length (or the height of your book).

2 Starting with the bookmark top, center the medium felt circle over the large fabric circle and appliqué stitch all the way around the edge. Now layer the small fabric circle over the medium felt circle and appliqué stitch around again. Do the same with the small fabric circle and one medium felt circle for the bottom of the bookmark.

3 Layer the remaining felt circles on the back of the appliquéd circles and blanket stitch all the way around the edge. For each end, insert the ribbon where you'd like and secure with a straight stitch before finishing the blanket stitch. Knot and tie on the back to finish.

Circle Bookmark

Instructions for the Heart Bookmark

1 Photocopy, enlarge and cut out all of the templates from heavy paper. Pin the large and small hearts to the felt and cut out one each. Cut one piece of patterned fabric using the large heart template. Cut one piece of ribbon to the desired length (or the height of your book).

2 Pin the small heart shape centered in the middle of the large fabric heart and work an appliqué stitch all the way around the edge. Sew an embellishment or button on top of the fabric if you wish.

3 Fold over the bottom of the ribbon and sew a small button to the folded end. Knot the thread on the back when finished.

4 Place the remaining felt heart on the back of the appliquéd heart piece and pin in place. Insert the end of the ribbon between the two felt pieces about 1" (2.5cm) into the bottom of the heart. Blanket stitch all the way around the edge and use straight stitches to tack the ribbon in place when you come to it. Knot and tie on the back when finished.

Heart Bookmark

Instructions for the Embroidery Hoop Mobile

Before you start, decide how you want to embellish each of the hoops. For my mobile, I created two hoops with framed fabric, one with lace, one with satin ribbon and one with a hanging fabric bauble. Once you're finished designing, lay out the hoops and decide the placement. Balance the larger and smaller hoops on each row so they hang evenly; you don't want one side to be too heavy.

1 (a & b) To create the framed fabric hoops, refer to the Patchworked Embroidery Hoops project (page 120) as a guide. I used two patterned fabrics for both of my fabric hoops: one for the front and the other for the back on one hoop, and the opposite on the second fabric hoop. Follow the same instructions for securing each framed hoop, with one exception: If another hoop will hang from it, cut a piece of embroidery floss to the desired length, tie several knots at one end, and slip it between the hoops before tightening the screw, leaving the thread hanging from the front. (Do this for any of the mobile's hoops that will have another hoop hanging from it.) On the large hoop, I attached two hanging threads since I hung two rows of hoops from it. Be sure to space them evenly and far enough apart that the hoops are free to spin when hanging.

2 For the lace hoop, cut several pieces of lace long enough to wrap around the inner hoop; then decide how you'd like to place the lace. I used several different colors and a simple basketweave design. Once you've decided on the design, smooth a thin layer of glue all the way around the outside edge of the inner hoop. Place the ribbons back on top of the inner hoop as desired and wrap them around the edge of the inner hoop, securing them with a little

more glue on the inside edge of your hoop. Then place the outer hoop over the inner and tighten the screw. Remember to place the hanging thread between the hoops if you are dangling another hoop from it.

3 For the ribbon hoop, I secured the ribbon in the same manner as the lace in step 2, but I used one long piece of ribbon and wrapped it randomly all the way around my inner hoop as tightly as possible until I created the desired effect. Secure the ends of the ribbon on the inside of the inner hoop with a bit of glue. Then place the outside hoop over the top and tighten the screw. Since this was a bottom hoop, it did not need a hanging thread at the bottom.

4 For the fabric bauble hoop, freehand cut a fun shape out of two different pieces of patterned fabric and straight stitch them together around the edge. Before finishing, add a little stuffing for shape and slip a piece of embroidery floss through the top of the bauble. Finish stitching the bauble closed. Then, tie and knot the floss around the inner hoop. Leave the thread long enough that the bauble dangles in the middle of the hoop; cut off any excess.

5 Secure the hoops together and finish the mobile. Slip the hanging threads from the top hoops underneath the screw of the embroidery hoop below. Wrap the floss around and tie several knots to hold it in place. Trim the excess floss. Repeat this step until all of the hoops are tied together in the layout that you choose.

6 Tie a piece of ribbon or lace to the top of the large hoop for hanging.

7 Hang from the ceiling to brighten up any room.

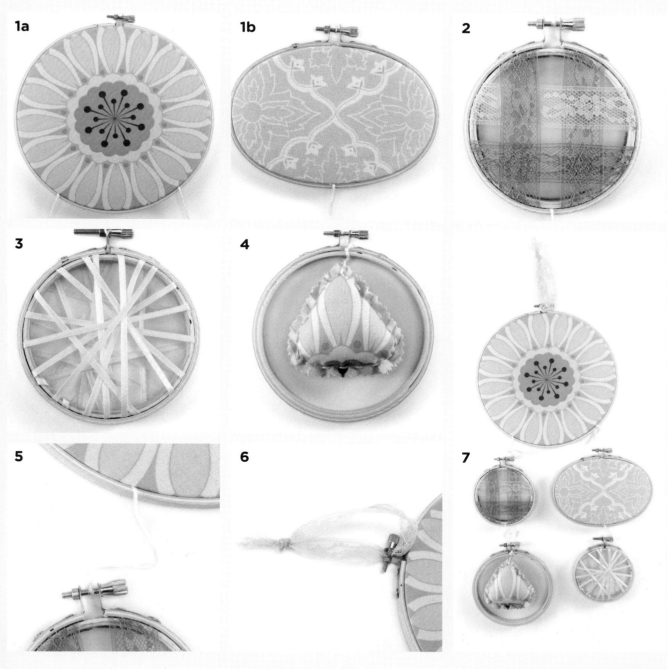

Embroidered Napkins and Napkin Rings

Some of my favorite vintage treasures are beautifully embroidered everyday items, such as napkins, hankerchiefs and pillowcases. Stitching sweet designs onto useful items like napkins is a great way to go green and embrace reusable napkins, while still making your meal, picnic or party extra special! Use kitchen-inspired designs, patterned fabric and embroidery to create these cheerful napkins and napkin rings. These would make a great housewarming gift!

Supplies for Embroidered Napkins:

• embroidery designs (page 139) • carbon tracing paper or transfer pencil • 2 pieces of light-colored patterned fabric, cut to 14½" x 13½" (36.8cm x 34.3cm) • a variety of embroidery floss • embroidery hoop • embroidery needle • scissors • tape measure or ruler • pins • sewing machine • iron

Supplies for Napkin Rings:

• template (page 139) • 1 small piece of white felt • 1 small piece of stiffened felt • several small buttons or other embellishments • 1' (0.3m) thin elastic cord • embroidery needle • scissors • tape measure or ruler • pins

Cute Cupcake Toppers

Make any occasion a memorable one with a fun batch of cupcake toppers. No matter what you're planning, you can bring your own individual touch to make an ordinary batch of cupcakes extraordinary with eight different cupcake toppers.

Supplies:

• embroidery design, templates (page 139) • a variety of small pieces of felt • small pieces of patterned fabrics • a variety of embroidery floss • lace • buttons and embellishments • stuffing • candy sticks • carbon tracing paper • felt glue and fabric glue • embroidery needle • scissors and pinking shears • tape measure or ruler • pins

Instructions for the Embroidered Napkins and Napkin Rings

To make one napkin:

1 Using carbon tracing paper or a transfer pencil, center a copy of your chosen embroidery designs on the front of one piece of patterned fabric and transfer the design. Use an embroidery hoop to keep the fabric taut, and stitch over the designs in a variety of embroidery floss colors. (I used a simple backstitch and straight stitch to complete my designs.)

2 Once the embroidery is complete, place the other fabric piece on top, right sides together. Line them up evenly and pin in place. Using 1/4" (6mm) seam allowance and a sewing machine (or a hand-sewn straight stitch), sew along all four edges, leaving a few inches (centimeters) open near the end.

3 Turn the napkin right side out, making sure to push all of the corners out fully. Run a hot iron over the entire napkin to make nice creases around each of the edges. Now fold the edges of the hole under to meet the crease, and pin in place. Stitch all the way around the edge, closing the hole as you go. When finished, pull the hanging thread in between the layers of fabric, and knot and tie on the reverse side. Go over the napkin again with a hot iron to smooth out all of the stitches.

To make one napkin ring:

4 Using the circle template (photocopied, enlarged and cut out from heavy paper), cut two from felt circles, one stiffened felt circle and one patterned fabric circle. Also cut one 3" (7.6cm) piece of elastic cording. Tie a knot at both ends of the elastic cording. Place one end of the elastic cording on one side of the stiffened felt circle so that the knot is close to the edge. Stitch down the cording by making tiny stitches over the cording on both sides of the knot. Repeat this step with the other end of the cording to form a loop behind the stiffened circle.

5 Embellish the fabric circle as desired. I embellished mine with small buttons; you might try adding another layer of fabric, a crocheted flower or a stitched design. Place a felt circle on either side of the stiffened felt and the fabric circle on top. Stitch all four circle layers together. Knot and tie the stitch on the back when finished, and your ring is ready for a napkin.

6 Slip the ring around the rolled napkin, set your table and serve.

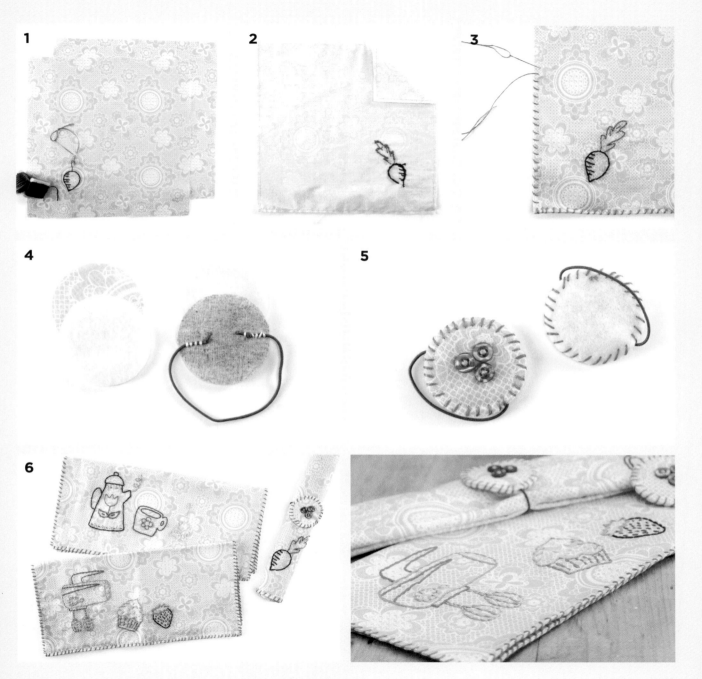

Instructions for the Cute Cupcake Toppers

Flag: Cut a 5" x 1½" (12.7cm x 3.8cm) strip of felt. Fold the strip in half and, where the ends meet, cut out a triangle shape (or use the flag template on page 139). Next, fold a 1½" (3.8cm) square of fabric in half and cut a triangle along the fold (this will look like a diamond when unfolded). Apply felt glue to one half of the unfolded felt flag and add a bit to the stick; then place the stick in the center and fold the flag over so that the ends meet. Using a small amount of fabric glue, adhere the fabric diamond to the flag so that a triangle shows on each side. Press firmly and allow to dry.

Button: Stitch a large button onto a felt square (larger than the button). Use pinking shears to cut around the outside of the button, leaving some space between the button and the edge. Place the buttoned felt on a piece of contrasting felt and cut so that the contrasting felt is showing. Straight stitch both pieces of felt together around the outside of the button, and knot and tie in the back. Push the stick in between the two layers of felt and up through the middle.

Crochet: Cut two small squares of felt, and place the crochet piece or other embellishment in the center of one. Stitch the embellishment in place using a long appliqué stitch. Put felt glue on the remaining felt piece and a bit on the stick. Glue the two felt pieces together with the stick sandwiched between them. Allow to dry.

Star: Cut two circles of felt about 2" (5.1cm) in diameter. Using a long straight stitch, make a simple star shape on one circle. Knot and tie on the back when finished. Put felt glue on the remaining felt piece and a bit on the stick. Glue the two felt pieces together with the stick sandwiched between them. Allow to dry.

Diamond: Cut out two felt diamond shapes. Trace the diamond embroidery design onto carbon tracing paper and pin it to the diamond shape. Use a backstitch to create the diamond. When finished, gently tear away the tracing paper. Glue the two felt pieces together with the stick sandwiched between them. Allow to dry.

Fabric Lollipop: Cut out a fabric circle about 4" (10.2cm) in diameter using pinking shears. Straight stitch all the way around the edge, about ½" (13mm) inside the edge. When finished, begin pulling on the hanging thread to cinch the circle together. Use your finger to press up through the middle before cinching it completely. Fill the shape with a small ball of stuffing. Place glue at the end of the stick and insert it into the hole. Cinch the fabric tightly around the stick, and knot and tie. Tie another piece of floss around the cinched part as tightly as you can, and knot and tie to finish.

Lace Flower: Cut a few pieces of lace in varying lengths from about 2" to 3" (5.1cm to 7.6cm) long, fold in half, and stack the folded pieces. Using a small piece of embroidery floss, tie the ends of the lace together around the top of the stick. Cut a 1" x 2" (2.5cm x 5.1cm) piece of felt with pinking shears. Place felt glue on one side of the felt and wrap it tightly around the top of the stick. Freehand cut a leaf shape and glue the very end to the bottom of the flower. Allow to dry.

Mini Patchwork: Cut four 1" (2.5cm) squares of fabric. Place two squares right sides together, stitch along one edge and press open. Repeat this with the other two squares. Place these sewn rectangles right sides together, sew along one long edge and press open. Cut a felt square the same size for the backing. Blanket stitch around the edges to join the patchwork and backing squares. Insert the stick in between two stitches in the bottom.

Flag

Button

Crochet

Star

Diamond

Fabric Lollipop

Lace Flower

Mini
Patchwork

Geometric Wall Tapestry

Bring a modern 1960's sensibility to your space with this bold geometric tapestry. With colorful repeating shapes and an understated design, you'll create a funky wall hanging that is sure to please the eye. This is the ideal project to add a punch of color and a bit of "retro" to your décor.

Supplies:

template (page 138) • cardboard or cardstock • 1 solid colored piece of fabric, cut to 22" x 17" (55.9cm x 43.2cm) • 21 different colors of felt • embroidery floss to match felt • ribbon • dowel rod • felt glue • embroidery needle • scissors • tape measure or ruler • pins

Felt Decorative Chains

Delightful felt decorative chains always bring smiles, whether you're having a celebration or making every day extra special! Hang some chains from your mantle, make chain curtains for your doorway or add them to your party décor.

Supplies:

7 felt sheets in various colors (1 felt sheet makes approximately 9 strips; 60" [152.4cm] of chain requires 60 felt strips) • cardboard or cardstock • embroidery floss • felt glue • embroidery needle • scissors • tape measure or ruler • pins

Instructions for the
Geometric Wall Tapestry

1 Photocopy, enlarge and cut out the hexagon template from heavy paper. Cut twenty-one hexagons and at least two half-hexagons from twenty-one colors of felt, and gather embroidery floss to match. You could also use fewer colors or different shades of one color.

2 Arrange the hexagons on top of the solid fabric in columns, using a half hexagon at the top of some columns so they appear staggered. Leave an even edge all the way around the tapestry and about 3″ to 4″ (7.6cm to 10.2cm) at the top to insert the dowel rod later. Once you have the design how you want it, pick up one hexagon at a time, add a small drop of felt glue to each of the shape's points, and press firmly back in place on the fabric. Let the shapes dry for an hour or two.

3 When the shapes are dry, use matching floss to straight stitch all the way around the edge of each hexagon.

4 Turn the base fabric over, fold over the edges and iron in place. Using floss that matches the solid-colored fabric, straight stitch around the edge on three sides, leaving the top unstitched.

5 Fold over the unstitched top of the tapestry, leaving enough room to insert the small dowel rod. Stitch along the raw edge to make a dowel pocket about 1″ (2.5cm) wide.

6 Insert the dowel rod through the pocket. Tie each end of a long ribbon to each end of the dowel rod.

7 Hang in a place of honor!

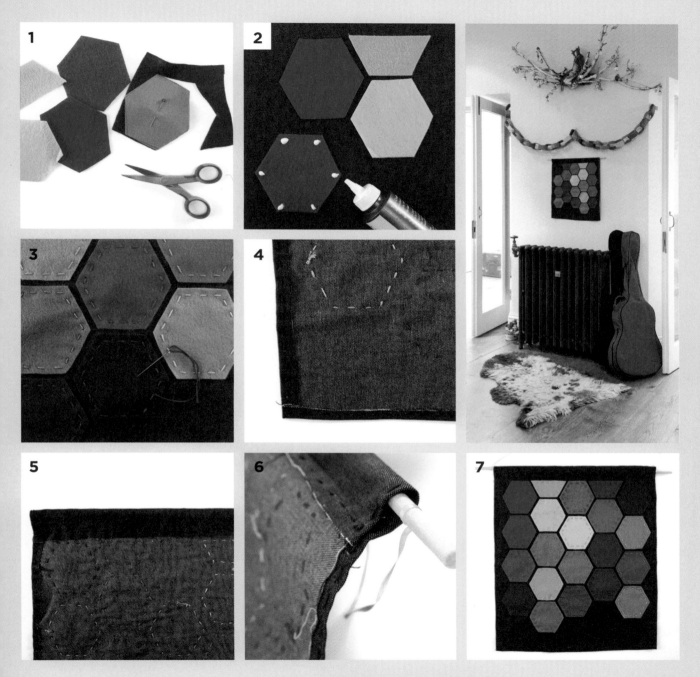

Instructions for the Felt Decorative Chains

1 Cut an 8" x 1¼" (20.3cm x 3.2cm) rectangle out of heavy paper to use as the template. Each link in the chain will require two strips of felt. One felt sheet will yield approximately nine strips of felt, and you will need about sixty strips to create a 60" (152.4cm) chain. For quicker cutting, make extra templates and pin them to the entire sheet of felt so when you are finished with one strip, you are ready to cut the next. Use at least two different colors of felt for each of the links (colors representing holidays, your favorite sports team, etc.), or use varying shades of one color for another neat effect.

2 Use felt glue to glue together the various strips of felt, alternating colors as the example shows or gluing two strips of the same color to make each link. Apply a thin line of glue close to each edge for almost the entire length of the strip, leaving about a ½" (13mm) at one end of the strip free of glue. Press another felt strip firmly on top to adhere them together. Let all strips dry before moving on to the next step.

3 To start making the chain, make a loop with the first felt strip. Sandwich the glued end in between the two layers of the unglued end. Sew three cross stitches to sew the ends together in a loop (stitch out from the inside of the link). Loop the next felt strip through the loop you just stitched closed. Sandwich the glued end between the unglued end layers, and complete the three cross stitches to close the link. Repeat until your chain is the desired length.

Nesting Doll, Owl and Fox Softies

I'm positive there isn't a person out there who didn't have a beloved softie growing up. Softies are for everyone, though, not just the kiddos! In fact, I'm not ashamed to admit I have a few adorable softies scattered around my crafty lab for inspiration, and because they're just plain cute. We'll make three cheerful softies together—a nesting doll, an owl, and a friendly fox—using hand sewing, bold felts and colorful patterned fabrics.

Supplies for nesting doll:

• templates (page 140) • cardboard or cardstock • 6 colors of felt (doll front, doll back/bonnet, face, hair, cheeks, mouth) • 1 small piece of patterned fabric • 5 colors of embroidery floss (matching doll back/bonnet, hair, cheeks, mouth, buttons) • 1 piece of small ribbon • stuffing • 2 buttons • embroidery needle • scissors • pins

Supplies for owl:

• templates (page 140) • cardboard or cardstock • 3 colors of felt (body, wings/eyes, beak) • 1 small piece of patterned fabric • 3 colors of embroidery floss (2 coordinating, 1 matching beak) • stuffing • 2 buttons • embroidery needle • scissors • pins

Supplies for fox:

• templates (page 140) • cardboard or cardstock • 3 colors of felt (body/tail color, white, black) • 1 small piece of patterned fabric • 3 colors of embroidery floss (1 coordinating, 1 pink for ears, 1 gray for nose) • stuffing • 2 buttons • embroidery needle • scissors and pinking shears • pins

101

Instructions for the Nesting Doll Softie

1 Photocopy, enlarge and cut out all of the templates from heavy paper. Cut a body front from one color of felt, a body back and bonnet (or babushka, as my Czech mother would say!) from a second color, and the big face, hair, two cheeks, and mouth from the desired colors.

Note: If you are using a light face color, cut out two face circles to layer, so the darker felt behind it won't show through.

To cut the circle from the bonnet where the face will be, center and pin the small face circle on the bonnet, and pinch the edge to make a small cut. Then slip your scissors into the small slit you've made and finish cutting out the shape. From patterned fabric (preferably thicker cotton), cut out the dress accent. (If using a thinner cotton, add weight with fusible interfacing, for easier sewing.)

2 Center and straight stitch the large face circle on the body front, and knot and tie off the thread. Place the hair piece over the face, and straight stitch along the bottom edge only. Center the fabric dress piece on the bottom of the body front, just under the face circle. Using an accent color of floss, straight stitch along the two top sides, and appliqué stitch along the bottom curve. Knot and tie off the thread on the back.

3 Place and pin the bonnet on the body front, lining up the sides. Straight stitch along the bottom edge only. Then straight stitch the inside circle around the face.

4 Straight stitch the rosy cheeks onto the doll's face. Stitch on the button eyes; if desired, add a few straight-stitch eyelashes around each button. Straight stitch the heart-shaped mouth in place.

With wrong sides together, pin the front to the back of the doll, carefully aligning the edges. Starting at the base of the head and working clockwise, blanket stitch the two body pieces together, leaving several inches open toward the end for stuffing. (For rounder shapes like this, I prefer to start stuffing at the bottom, work around the edges, and then finish the middle.) When you are almost done stuffing the head, add a few more blanket stitches, and then stuff some more. Repeat until the head is stuffed fully. Finish the blanket stitch by wrapping the thread through the beginning stitch and bringing it between the two layers of felt. Knot and tie off the thread in the back.

5 Tie a small ribbon around the doll's neck to finish.

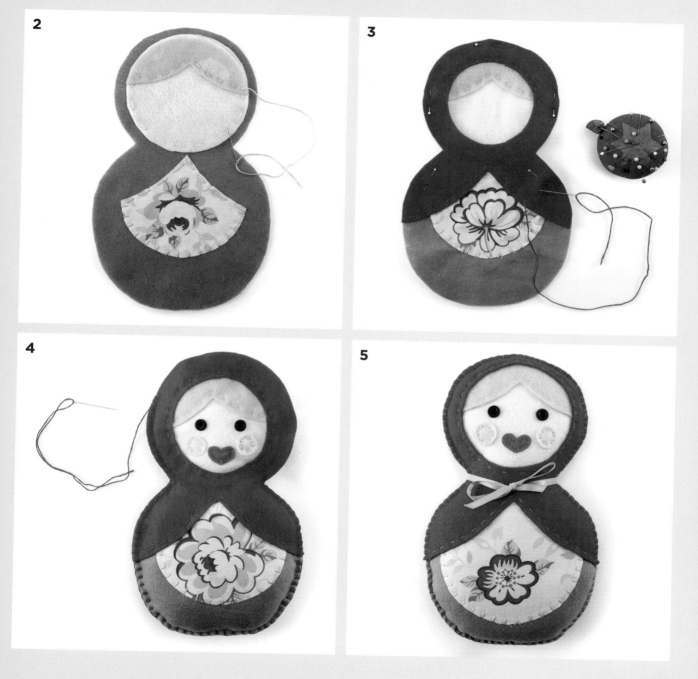

Instructions for the Owl Softie

1 Photocopy, enlarge and cut out all of the templates from heavy paper. Cut a body front and back from one color of felt, two wings and two large eye circles from a second color, and a beak from a third color. From patterned fabric, cut out the chest piece and one small eye. Center the fabric chest piece on the owl front, wrapping 1" (2.5cm) of fabric around the bottom of the felt, and pin it in place. Starting at the bottom of one side, straight stitch up to the top of the fabric. Once you reach the top, appliqué stitch over to the other side, then straight stitch down to the bottom. Knot and tie off the thread on the back.

2 Place the wings on the body front, lining them up along the edges, and pin in place. Straight stitch along the rounded inner edge of each wing. Knot and tie off the thread on the back. Place and pin the felt eye circles on the owl, about ½" (13mm) in from each edge. Straight stitch around each circle, and knot and tie off the thread on the back.

3 Center and pin the small fabric eye on one felt eye. Appliqué stitch around the edge of the fabric circle. Center the felt beak piece and straight stitch along three edges. Then stuff the beak with a small amount of stuffing. When you are finished stuffing, straight stitch along the last side of the beak. Knot and tie off the thread on the back.

4 Stitch a pupil button on each of the eyes, making sure to center both buttons the same way on each eye circle. After stitching them on, knot and tie off your thread on the back. With wrong sides together, pin your completed owl front to the owl back piece, carefully aligning the edges. Starting at the bottom center of your owl, blanket stitch the two body pieces together, leaving several inches open toward the end.

Begin stuffing the owl, at the top and around the edges first, then in the middle. When the owl is almost stuffed completely, blanket stitch down the edge a little more and then stuff a bit more if needed. Repeat until the owl is fully stuffed.

5 Finish the blanket stitch by wrapping the thread through the beginning stitch and bringing it between the two layers of felt. Knot and tie off the thread in the back.

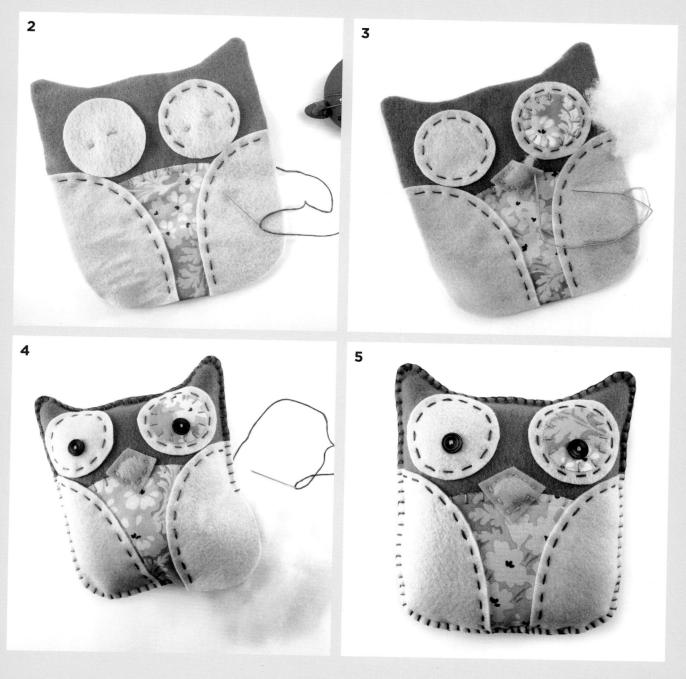

Instructions for the Fox Softie

1 Photocopy, enlarge and cut out all of the templates from heavy paper. Cut out a body front, a body back, a tail front, a tail back, and a tuft from the same color of felt. Cut out a cheek piece and a tail accent from white felt, and a nose from black felt. Cut out a belly piece from patterned fabric. Center the belly piece on the fox front, wrapping 1" (2.5cm) of fabric around the bottom of the felt, and pin it in place. Appliqué stitch up one side and around to the other, but not the bottom edge (we'll do that later). Pin the cheek piece in place, and straight stitch across the top and bottom (ignore the sides, which we'll stitch later). Straight stitch the tuft of fur onto the head, leaving the top unstitched.

Now find the front tail piece and tail accent piece. Cut across the bottom of the accent piece with pinking shears. Position and pin the accent piece to the top of the tail, and cross stitch along the bottom of the accent piece just above the decorative edge. Stitch a few open zigzag stitches along the top side of the tail.

2 Position and straight stitch the nose in place. Knot and tie off the thread on the back. Position and pin the front tail piece along the side of the front body piece, lining them up along the bottom. Straight stitch from the bottom of the tail up to the end of the body.

1

3 Attach the back tail piece to the back body piece in the same way as the front tail and body pieces in step 2, but on the opposite side of the body in a reverse image. Be sure to line them up carefully so that they will come together evenly with the front pieces.

4 Use three straight stitches to add detail to each ear. Sew on the button eyes. With wrong sides together, position and pin the front and back body/tail pieces. Straight stitch them together from the base of the head on the right to the base of the head on the other side. Begin stuffing the fox, starting with the point of the tail and along all of the edges. Then stuff the middle and work up to the base of the head. Then complete some more straight stitches and keep stuffing.

5 Keep stitching and stuffing until you arrive back at the beginning stitch. Knot and tie off the thread on the back of the fox.

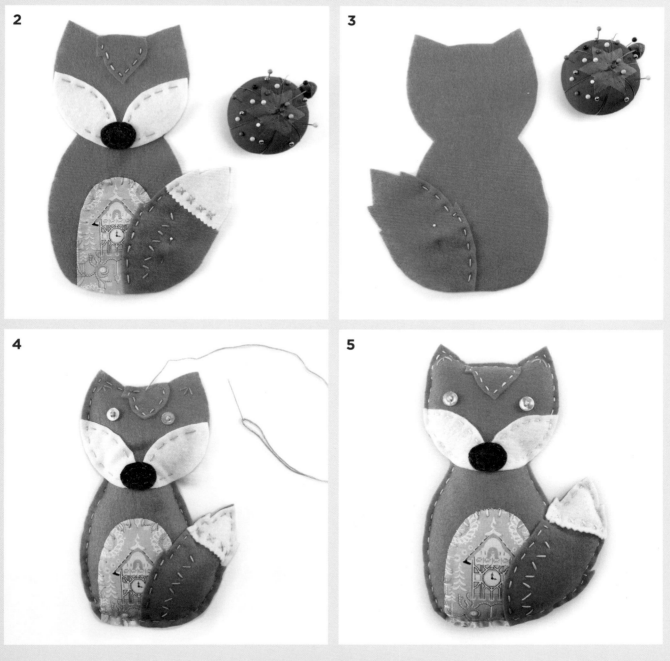

Anytime Ornaments

Nature lovers will adore this sweet little collection of everyday ornaments. Great for anytime gifts or adding a bit of cute, this collection is sure to delight. We'll make a bird, bull and snail from felt, and embroider a birdhouse, flower pot and tree to go with them.

Supplies:

• templates and embroidery designs (page 141) • carbon tracing paper or transfer pencil • 1 small piece of canvas fabric in white or natural • 11 colors of felt (4 for bird, 3 each for bull and snail, 1 for embroidery ornament backing) • variety of embroidery floss • ribbon • small buttons • stuffing • felt glue • embroidery hoop • embroidery needle • scissors

Instructions for the Anytime Ornaments

Making the Embroidered Ornaments

1 Cut a small square of canvas for each of the ornaments, large enough to fit in the embroidery hoop. Using carbon tracing paper or transfer pencil, transfer the embroidery designs to the fabric.

2 Place the fabric into the embroidery hoop and use a back stitch to sew over the designs. Use the colors that you'd like for each of the designs to transform them into colorful line drawings. Once you have all of the designs stitched, remove them from the hoop and cut around each of the designs, leaving about a ½" (13mm) edge.

3 Pin the fabric designs on top of the ornmanet backing felt. Using the designs as templates, cut closely around the ornament edges. Cut three pieces of ribbon, fold the ribbons in half, and tie the ends together to make a loop for each ornament. Tuck the knotted ends in between the felt and fabric layers at the top of the ornament. Sew each ornament front to its backing felt, straight stitching all the way around the edge. Double the stitch when you come to the ribbon at the top, and leave a bit open for stuffing.

4 Add enough stuffing to give form, and then finish stitching the ornament closed. Knot and tie on the back.

1

2

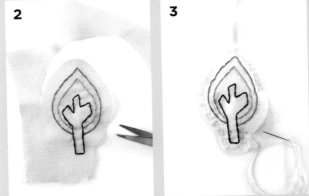

3

4

Making the Felt Ornaments

Photocopy, enlarge and cut out all of the templates from heavy paper. Pin each to the desired color of felt and cut out all of the shapes, cutting out two each for the main body shapes of each animal so that you have a backing. Cut one additional circle for the snail in a contrasting color. Also tie a piece of ribbon into a loop for each ornament.

For the bird ornament:

1 On one bird body, sew a small button for the eye, and add one teardrop wing shape using a few straight stitches for the wing. On the second bird body, straight stitch the three other teardrop tailfeather shapes at the point of the tail. Freehand cut a small felt triangle for the beak and position it in place on the second bird body.

2 Place and pin the first bird body over the second, and sandwich the ribbon in between the layers at the top for hanging. Straight stitch starting at the bottom center of the bird and working all the way around. Double the stitches when you come to the ribbon at the top, and leave a bit open at the bottom for stuffing.

3 Lightly stuff the bird, and then finish stitching the ornament closed. Knot and tie on the back.

For the snail ornament:

1 Sew a small button at the front of the skinny snail body piece. Place the two skinny body pieces together and pin. Straight stitch most of the way around the edge, leaving a bit open for stuffing. Lightly stuff the body piece and complete the straight stitch. Next, take the contrasting circle piece and, beginning from the outside edge, cut a freehand spiral all the way to the center of the piece. Open the spiral a bit and place it on top of one felt shell circle. Straight stitch the spiral in place in a contrasting floss color. Knot and tie on the back when finished.

2 To make antennae, cut two small pieces of floss and tie a knot at the end. Starting from the back of the snail body, bring the floss through the two layers of felt and out of the top, above the eye. Tie a knot at the top of each thread so that they pop out of the top.

Pin the second shell circle to the front shell, with the snail body tucked slightly in between the circles. Place the ribbon loop at the top in between the circles. Straight stitch all the way around the edge, doubling up when you come to the ribbon and stitching all the way through the snail body. Leave a small section open for stuffing.

3 Stuff the snail's shell and then complete the straight stitch. Knot and tie on the back.

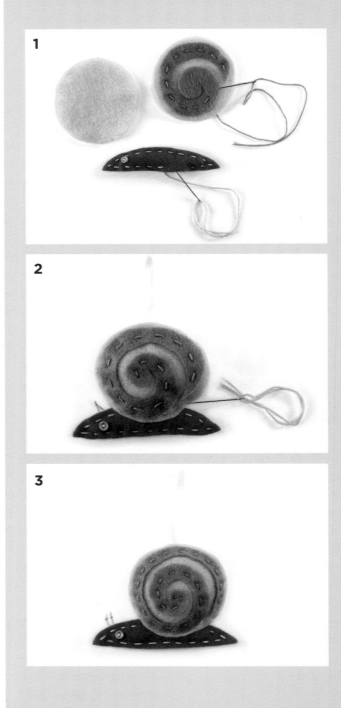

For the bull ornament:

1 Freehand cut a small circle shape from contrasting felt for the bull's muzzle. Place it on one of the bull head shapes and straight stitch all the way around the edge. Make two vertical straight stitches side by side for the nostrils. Using yellow or gold floss and small backstitches, sew the bull's nose ring. Stitch two small buttons on the head for the eyes. Next, freehand cut two small teardrop shapes for the ears.

2 Place the second bull head on the back of the first, the looped ribbon at the top bewteen the layers, and the horns and ears on the side between the layers. Sew a straight stitch all the way around the edge, doubling up when you come to the ribbon, and leaving a bit open for stuffing.

3 Lightly stuff the bull, and then finish stitching the ornament closed. Knot and tie on the back.

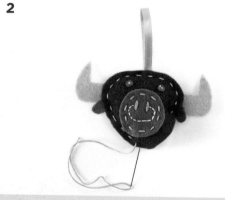

Sewing Room Wall Organizer

If you're always searching for that pair of scissors or those spare buttons, then put this wall organizer on your project to-do list. It's so easy to complete your crafting projects when all of your tools are handy and easily accessible. This cute project is inspired by all things sewing. Use felt and fabric to create a fun, bobbin-shaped organizer with plenty of pockets to house your crafty goodies.

Supplies:

• templates (page 141) • cardboard or cardstock • 3 pieces of tan felt, cut to 18″ x 16″ (45.7cm x 40.6cm) • 6 colors of felt for appliqués • embroidery floss to match the appliqués, plus 1 accent color • ½ yard (0.5m) of striped or patterned fabric • thick ribbon • rickrack and matching thread • stuffing • embroidery needle • scissors • tape measure or ruler • pins • iron

Instructions for the Sewing Room Wall Organizer

1 Photocopy, enlarge and cut out all of the templates from heavy paper. From various colors of felt, cut two thimbles, two buttons, four button holes, four floss bobbins, two rectangles (bobbin floss) from different colors, two tomatoes, and one leafy top. (The floss bobbins, thimble and button will become pockets, so we want them to be sturdy.)

From the tan felt, cut an 18″ x 16″ (45.7cm x 40.6cm) rectangle. Fold the rectangle in half lengthwise and begin cutting a rounded edge about 1″ (2.5cm) into the shape. Continue cutting a straight line until you get close to the top, and then form another rounded edge about 2″ (5.1cm) from the top. Once you have the desired shape, pin it to the other piece of matching felt and cut a second bobbin shape.

Using the photos for reference, cut an oval shape from the tan felt that matches the curved upper edge of the bobbin shape you just cut, and rounds off at the bottom (like a hot dog).

Next cut two approximately 16″ x 16″ (40.6cm x 40.6cm) pieces of patterned fabric. Fold and press under the top and bottom edges of the fabric so the fabric is as tall as the narrow part of the felt bobbin. Also cut a 16″ x 7″ (40.6cm x 17.8cm) piece of patterned fabric.

2 The smaller piece of patterned fabric will become the pocket. Fold and press the top and bottom long edges under (toward the wrong side) two times to completely conceal the raw edges. Then stitch rickrack along the top of the pocket using matching thread.

3 Center the large piece of patterned fabric on top of one felt bobbin. Next place the pocket fabric on top, bottom edges aligned. Fold and pin the fabric around the edges of the bobbin so the fabric is flush with the sides of the bobbin. With the accent floss, straight stitch along the bottom of the pocket, and then stitch two vertical lines from the bottom edge to the top of the pocket to create pocket dividers.

4 Now it's time to work on the appliqués. For the pincushion, center the leafy top on the top of one tomato. Straight stitch along the bottom leaves only to secure it in place. Straight stitch two arched lines on the tomato to add detail.

Next, straight stitch the four small circles to one of the button shapes. Layer the two large button shapes on top of each other, straight stitch halfway around the button and set it aside.

On one of the thimble shapes, straight stitch a few rows along the bottom and top of the thimble, and add some random open loop stitches. Layer the two thimble shapes on top of each other, straight stitch around the top of the thimble only, and then knot and tie on the back.

Center each colored felt rectangle on a floss bobbin. Using matching floss, stitch random long and short stitches through each square to resemble the look of a wound bobbin. Overlap the bobbins at a slight angle and straight stitch along the edge of the floss rectangle to hold the two bobbins together. Overlap and stitch the two remaining floss bobbins to match the front bobbin piece. Layer the front and back floss bobbin pieces, and straight stitch along the top only. Knot and tie when finished. (continued on page 118)

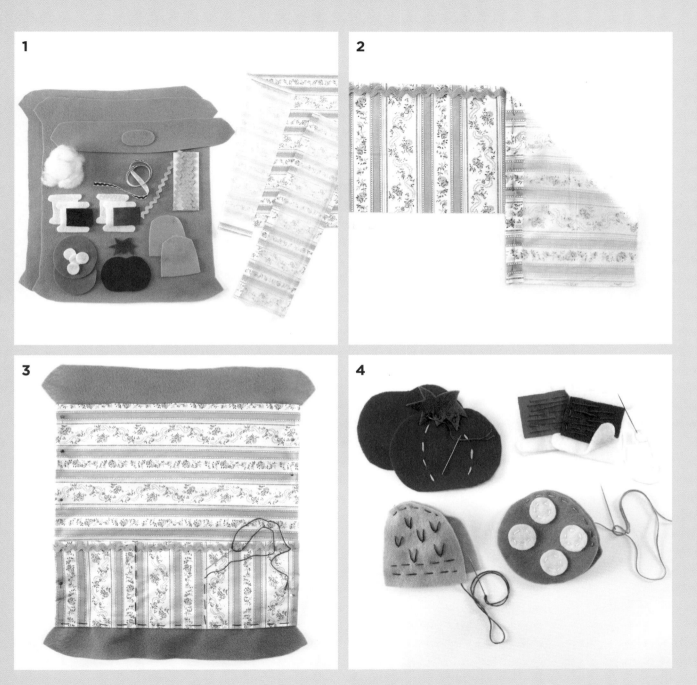

5 Pin the tomato where you'd like it on the organizer front, and finish stitching the leaves through the bobbin piece and fabric to secure in place. Then stitch around the edge of the tomato, pausing near the end to stuff the tomato lightly. After stuffing, finish stitching around the tomato, and knot and tie the thread on the back.

Next, pin the thimble in place. Straight stitch the thimble to the organizer front along the sides and bottom of the thimble, leaving the top unstitched to create the pocket. Knot and tie on the back. Now place the button and finish stitching it together through the bobbin to form a button pocket. Knot and tie the thread on the back.

Position and pin the floss bobbins to the organizer next. Using matching bobbin floss, stitch the floss bobbins to the organizer along both sides and the bottom, leaving the floss top unstitched to create the pocket. Knot and tie the thread on the back. Now all of the pockets are complete.

6 Pin the large tan oval you cut in step 1 to the top of the organizer front, overlapping the patterned fabric and aligning all outside edges. Straight stitch along the bottom of the oval. Next, freehand cut a small oval out of matching felt and straight stitch it to the center of the large oval. Now pin the second large tan felt bobbin to the back of the organizer front, and straight stitch the bottom of the organizer together—from one rounded edge to the other. (You'll do the sides of the bobbin last.) Next, sandwich and pin two looped ribbons between the front and back pieces of the organizer. Straight stitch the top of the organizer together, doubling your stitch when you reach the ribbons.

7 Using the accent floss from the bottom of the pocket, sew both sides of the organizer together.

8 Hang your sewing-inspired organizer in your sewing room, place your favorite gadgets in the pockets and enjoy your organized work space!

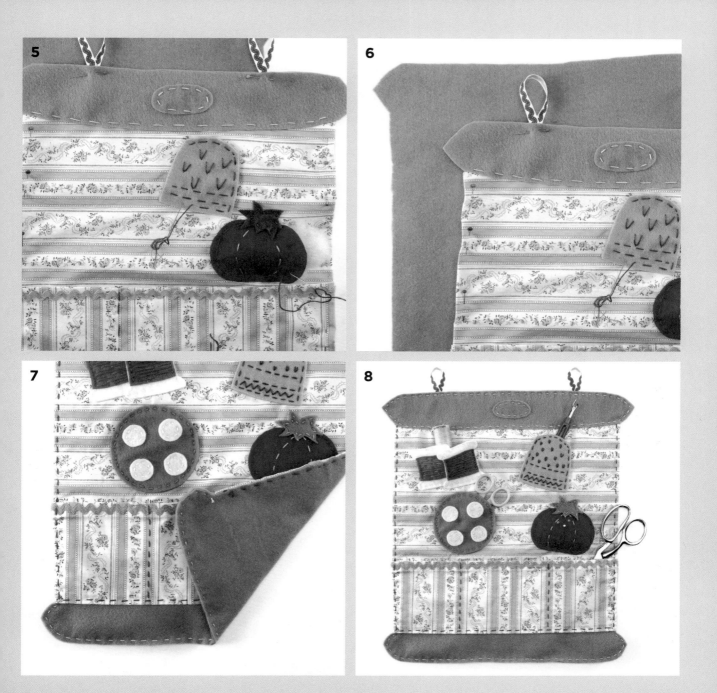

Scrapbook Embellishments

If you're short on flair and need a little extra adornment, whip up one of these super-quick embellishments for your next scrapbook layout, gift or other crafty creation. Use felt and scrap fabric to create some abstract flowers, a cute paisley and a special yo-yo to add a little something special to any project.

Supplies:

• templates (page 141) • cardboard or cardstock • 2 colors of felt • a variety of fabric scraps • a variety of embroidery floss • ribbon • buttons • embroidery needle • scissors and pinking shears • tape measure or ruler • pins

Patchworked Embroidery Hoops

Patchwork has been around for centuries, but we can make it modern by piecing together a variety of pretty fabrics and embellishments. Create these hip patchwork hoops to add a bit of texture to your wall displays, or, for a splash of color and pattern, make a whole set to adorn your space.

Supplies:

• a variety of embroidery hoops in any size • a variety of fabric scraps • 1 solid colored piece of fabric, at least 1" (2.5cm) larger than your hoop • various embellishments: buttons, ribbon, lace, sequins, beads • embroidery floss • quick-drying craft glue • embroidery needle • scissors • sewing machine • tape measure or ruler • pins

Instructions for the Scrapbook Embellishments

For the abstract flower:

1 Cut out a circle of felt about 2" (5.1cm) in diameter. Freehand cut a bunch of petals from a few different fabrics using pinking shears.

2 Layer all of the petals in a circular fashion on top of the felt circle. Once you've got a placement that you like, cut a smaller felt circle with pinking shears and place it on top of the petals.

3 Using embroidery floss, stitch around the center felt circle to hold all of the petals in place. Make a few more rows of straight stitches in different colors and add a button to become the center of the flower.

4 Use this pretty flower on any scrapbook layout that could use a colorful embellishment.

Abstract Flower

For the funky yo-yo:

1 Cut a circle of fabric about 4" (10.2cm) in diameter. With the wrong side up, straight stitch close to the edge all the way around the circle. When finished, pull the end so that it gathers. Press the yo-yo in the center and straighten it out around the middle so that it is even on all edges. Gather tightly in the center and knot and tie.

2 Cut a few pieces of ribbon a bit smaller than the width of the yo-yo and cross them at the center.

3 Find a cute button and, from the back, stitch through the yo-yo and ribbons to sew the button in place. Knot and tie on the back when finished.

4 These are perfect to use on a scrapbook page with a girlie theme!

Funky Yo-Yo

For the paisley piece:

1 Photocopy, enlarge and cut out the paisley templates from heavy paper. Cut the larger shape out of felt and the inside shape out of fabric. Using the pinking shears, cut another large paisley out of a different colored felt, leaving a bit of room around the edge.

2 Place the small fabric paisley on top of the medium felt paisley, and use an appliqué stitch to sew in place. Add some decorative stitches to the center of the fabric when you are finished.

3 Now layer the felt paisley on top of the jagged paisley. Straight stitch around the edge to hold it in place. For extra flair, stitch a button on to the end of the paisley if you'd like.

4 Use these pailseys to embellish a more masculine scrapbook layout.

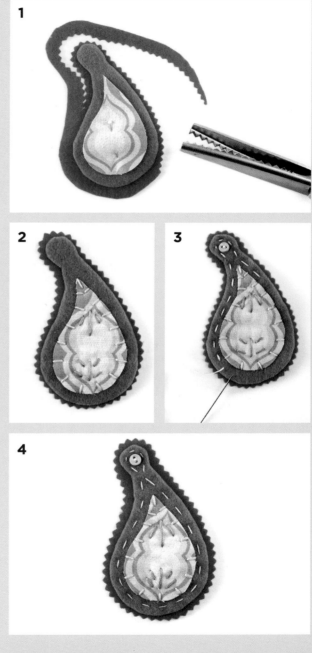

123

Instructions for the Patchworked Embroidery Hoops

1 Cut and sew together various sizes of squares and rectangles for the patchwork. Keep adding fabric to form a square shape that is large enough for the embroidery hoop and has at least 1" (2.5cm) excess around the outside of the hoop.

2 Place the patchwork fabric in the embroidery hoop. Add a bit of extra interest to the patchwork by lining the seams with various embroidery stitches in a variety of floss colors. Add buttons and other embellishments, if desired.

3 Take the completed patchwork out of the embroidery hoop and separate the hoop. Center the piece of solid fabric over the inner hoop, with the wrong side of the fabric facing you. This will become the backing fabric. Now place the patchwork right side up on top of the backing fabric. Place the outside hoop on top and tighten the screw. Pull gently around all sides of the fabric so that everything is tight. Using a small pair of scissors, trim only the backing fabric as close to the hoop as possible. Then trim down the patchwork using the hoop as your guide, leaving about a ½" (13mm) outside of the hoop to fold over the edge.

4 Place a line of glue a quarter of the way along the back embroidery hoop. Fold the fabric over the glue and press down for a few moments until the glue begins to stick. Repeat this step, working all the way around the hoop.

5 Follow these steps again to make a whole set of eclectic framed hoops!

Embellishment Ideas
Gather up any extra embellishments, such as buttons, ribbons, lace, sequins, beads and embroidery floss. Sew on sequins to accent some bright and cheery spots of the patterned fabric. Stitch on letter beads to create an inspiring phrase. Incorporate little groupings of buttons on the fabric. Using the floss, string a few beads and secure to the patchwork. Anything goes!

1

2

3

4

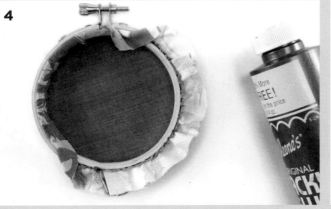

5

Simple Holiday Goodies

Holidays help make each year special. They're a time for sharing, gift giving, gathering, and spending time with family and friends. Sharing your handmade goodies will help spread a little love during the holiday seasons. Just make a few quick and easy decorations and doodads to celebrate Christmas, Halloween, Thanksgiving and the arrival of Spring!

Supplies for Christmas:

• templates (page 141) • cardboard or cardstock • 3 colors of felt (red, pink, green) • ribbon • white embroidery floss • embroidery needle • scissors • tape measure or ruler • pins

Supplies for Autumn/Thanksgiving:

• templates (page 141) • cardboard or cardstock • 4 colors of felt (gold, orange, deep red, brown) • matching embroidery floss • ribbon • earring hooks and jump rings • embroidery needle • scissors • tape measure or ruler • pins

Supplies for Halloween:

• templates (page 141) • cardboard or cardstock • 5 colors of felt (dark purple or black, green, white, yellow, orange) • embroidery floss in purple, yellow, orange and white • stuffing • felt glue • embroidery needle • scissors and pinking shears • tape measure or ruler • pins

Supplies for Spring/Easter:

• templates (page 141) • cardboard or cardstock • 2 colors of felt (natural or bunny color, purple) • embroidery floss in white, yellow, pink, purple and mint • $3/4$" (2mm) pom-poms in bright colors • stuffing • embroidery needle • scissors • pins

Instructions for the
Simple Holiday Goodies

Christmas Goodies

Mini Rag Wreath: Cut a circle about 3" (7.6cm) in diameter from thick cardstock or heavy paper, and then cut a ½" (13mm) hole out of the center. Cut long, thin pieces of felt (about 6" x ¼" [15.2cm x 6mm]) in red, pink and green. Begin tying the strands of felt closely together around the paper wreath, knotting along the outside edge. Push the strands together as you go so that no paper is showing, until the wreath is entirely covered. Trim the strands to about 1" (5.1cm) long. Tie a ribbon through the center and knot the ends for hanging.

Mini Rag
Wreath

Mini Stocking: Photocopy, enlarge and cut out the stocking template from heavy paper. Cut two stockings (for the front and back) from red felt. Freehand cut two small diamond shapes and a ½" x 3" (13mm x 7.6cm) strip of felt from the other felt colors. Place and star stitch the diamonds on one stocking piece, working through the same point in the center of the diamond. Pin the other stocking piece to the back of the first piece. Fold the small felt strip in half and place it between the two stocking pieces along the top. Straight stitch all the way around the edge. This makes a cute little decoration or ornament. You can also leave the top open to stuff with treats or to use as a mini gift bag.

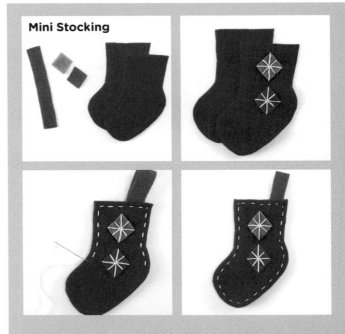

Mini Stocking

Autumn/Thanksgiving Goodies

Autumn Leaf Earrings: Photocopy, enlarge and cut out the leaf earring template from heavy paper. Cut two leaf earring pieces each from two different autumn-colored felts. On one each of the two different colors, stitch a few straight stitches down the center and out to the points in the leaves. Knot and tie off the thread on the back. Pin the remaining leaf shapes to the backs and straight stitch all the way around the edges of both leaves. To attach the hardware, open the jump ring and place the earring hook through it. Place the jump ring between the layers of felt and underneath one of the stitches, and then close the ring. Repeat for the other earring.

Autumn Pot Holder: Photocopy, enlarge and cut out the leaf templates from heavy paper. Cut out each leaf from a different autumn-colored felt, and cut three different 6½″ (16.5cm) squares. Place and pin the felt leaves on top of one square. Using a different floss color for each, make a few straight stitches up the center and to the points in the leaves. Continue the straight stitch around the edges of all of the leaves so that they are appliquéd to the square. Place the remaining two felt squares on the back and pin in place. Cut a small piece of ribbon and tie a knot, securing the ends together. Place the ribbon between the layers of felt at one of the corners. Straight stitch through all three layers of felt all the way around the edge and through the ribbon. Use detail scissors to round the corners a bit.

Leaf Earrings

Pot Holder

Halloween Goodies

Felt Ghost: With pinking shears, cut an 8″ (20.3cm) square. Cut a long piece of purple embroidery floss and straight stitch a circle about 3½″ to 4″ (8.9cm to 10.2cm) wide in the center of the square. Pull the end of the floss so that the stitches begin to gather. Place your thumb in the middle of the circle to push it outward. Leave a little room before cinching up completely and stuff the circle. Once the head is full, cinch the stitches as tightly as you can and tie a knot. Wrap another long piece of thread around the base of the head twice, and then knot. Cut four tiny felt rectangles. Use felt glue to adhere the rectangles as X's on the head for eyes. Stitch a long length of contrasting thread through the top and tie the ends together for hanging.

Felt Ghost

Candy Corn Treat Bag: Photocopy, enlarge and cut out all of the templates from heavy paper. Cut two pieces of the full shape out of white felt, one yellow top and one orange middle. Cut a 5″ x 1″ (12.7cm to 2.5cm) felt strip for the handle. Place the orange piece in the center of the candy corn, matching up the sides, and straight stitch along the bottom only with orange floss. Place the yellow top overlapping the orange, and straight stitch the bottom only with yellow floss. Pin the remaining full candy corn shape onto the back. Sew the two orange sides together with orange floss and the bottom point with white floss. Place one end of the handle between the layers of felt at the top of the candy corn. Sew along the front piece only with yellow floss, securing the yellow top and the handle end; leave the back unstitched and the top open. Secure the other end of the handle to the back with a few stitches.

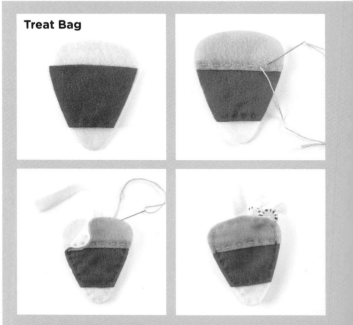

Treat Bag

Spring/Easter Goodies

Mini Bunny Plush: Photocopy, enlarge and cut out all of the templates from heavy paper. Cut two of the bunny shapes out of natural- or bunny-colored felt, and one tummy circle from purple felt. Straight stitch the tummy circle on the bottom of one felt bunny shape. For the face, make two small, vertical straight stitches for the eyes, and then stitch a triangle with pink floss for the nose. Add a few small, pink straight stitches in the ears. Now pin the other bunny shape to the back and, starting at the bottom, straight stitch most of the way around the edge. When you are almost finished, stuff lightly for shape, leaving the ears unstuffed. Stitch the bunny closed, and knot and tie off the thread on the back.

Mini Plush Bunny

Jelly Bean Garland: This one is super simple but super cute! Thread a long piece of embroidery floss through the center of the pom-poms, leaving a small space between each. When you have used the desired amount of pom-poms or reached the desired length, tie the ends together for a fun, playful party necklace. Or use a long strand as a springtime garland.

Jelly Bean Garland

Templates

Owl Gadget Cozy (Shown at 50%; Enlarge at 200%)

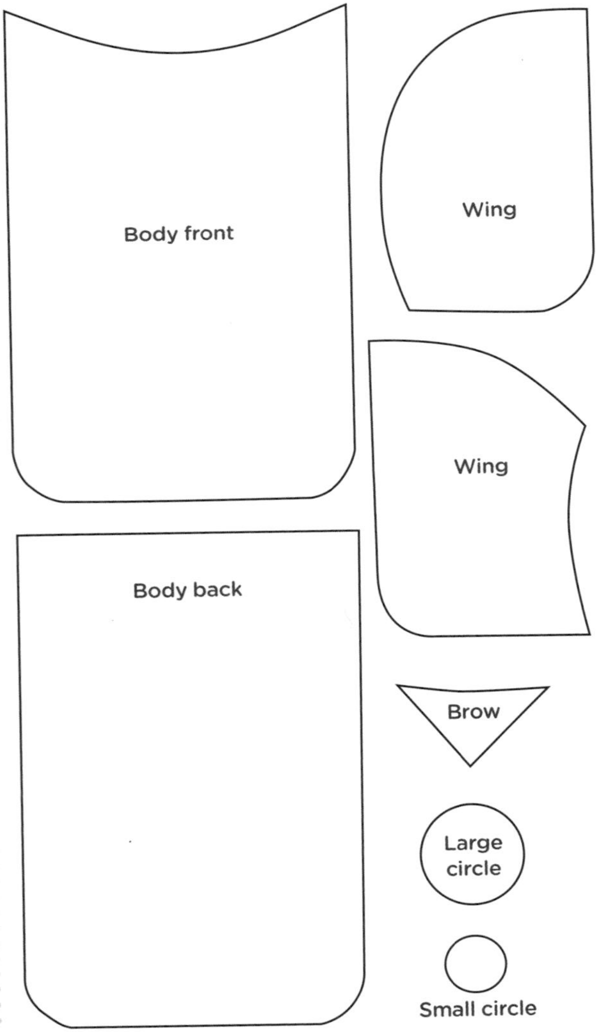

Body front

Wing

Wing

Body back

Brow

Large circle

Small circle

Row House Cozy (Shown at 25%; Enlarge at 200%, then enlarge at 200% again)

Roof (pointed)

Windows (half circle, rectangular, rounded)

Roof (scalloped)

Door (rounded top, rectangular)

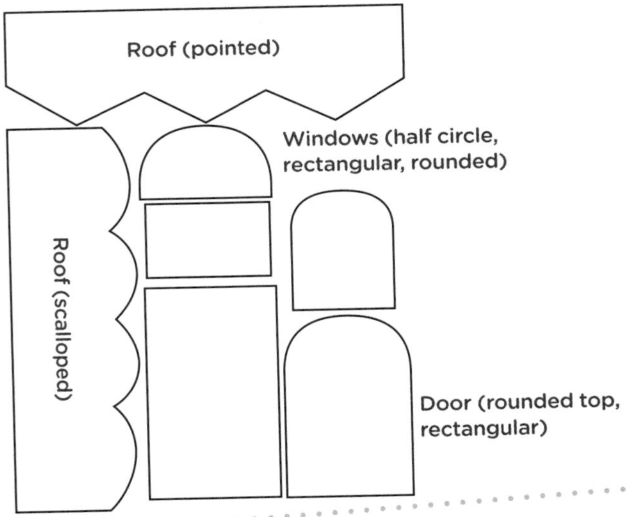

Monster Face Computer Cover (Shown at 25%; Enlarge at 200%, then enlarge at 200% again)

Eye

Large eye circle

Nose

Eyelash

Mouth

Mouth

Medium eye circle

Eye

Mouth

Small eye circle

Tooth and Nose

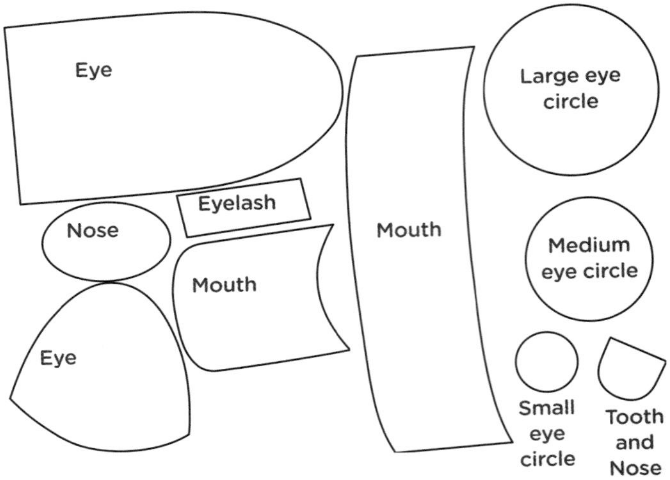

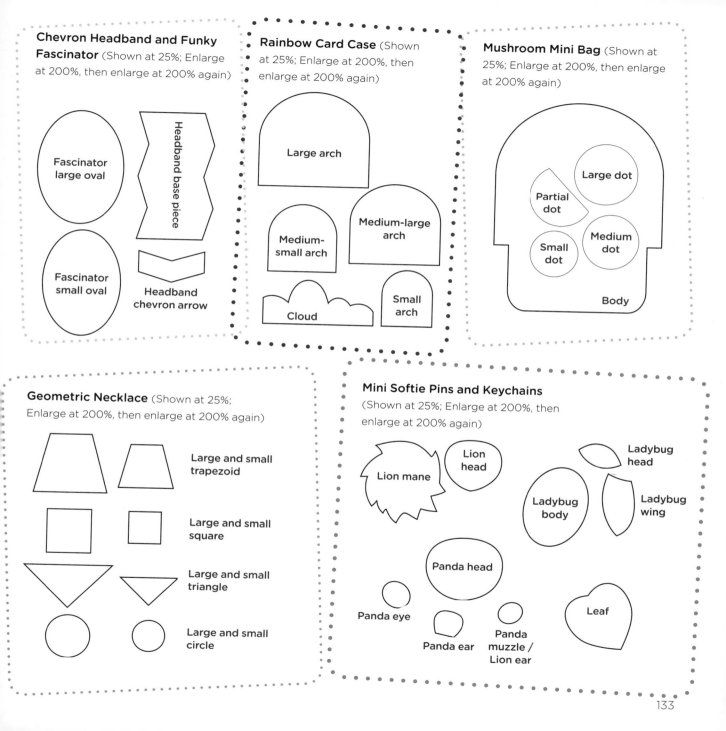

Chevron Headband and Funky Fascinator (Shown at 25%; Enlarge at 200%, then enlarge at 200% again)

Fascinator large oval

Fascinator small oval

Headband base piece

Headband chevron arrow

Rainbow Card Case (Shown at 25%; Enlarge at 200%, then enlarge at 200% again)

Large arch

Medium-small arch

Medium-large arch

Cloud

Small arch

Mushroom Mini Bag (Shown at 25%; Enlarge at 200%, then enlarge at 200% again)

Partial dot

Large dot

Small dot

Medium dot

Body

Geometric Necklace (Shown at 25%; Enlarge at 200%, then enlarge at 200% again)

Large and small trapezoid

Large and small square

Large and small triangle

Large and small circle

Mini Softie Pins and Keychains (Shown at 25%; Enlarge at 200%, then enlarge at 200% again)

Lion mane

Lion head

Ladybug head

Ladybug body

Ladybug wing

Panda head

Panda eye

Panda ear

Panda muzzle / Lion ear

Leaf

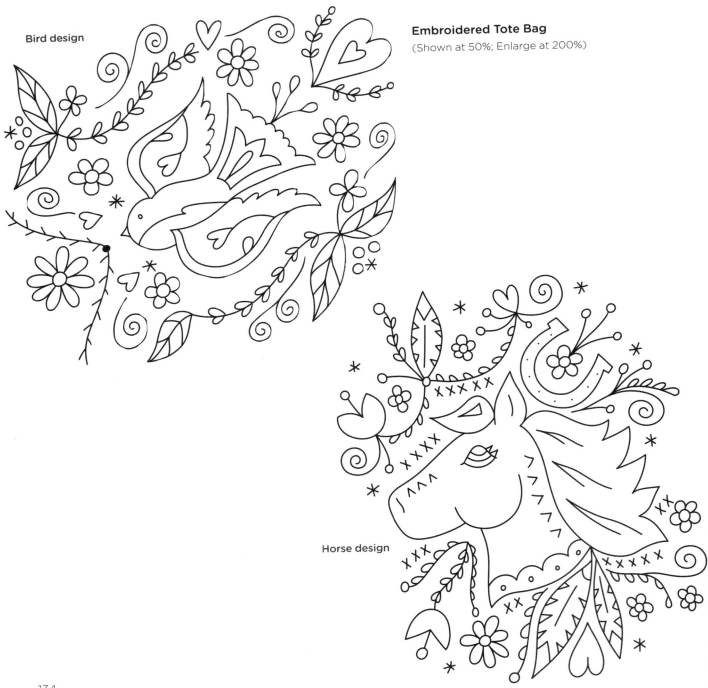

Bird design

Embroidered Tote Bag
(Shown at 50%; Enlarge at 200%)

Horse design

Denim Doodle Skirt

(Shown at 50%; Enlarge at 200%)

Doodle embroidery designs

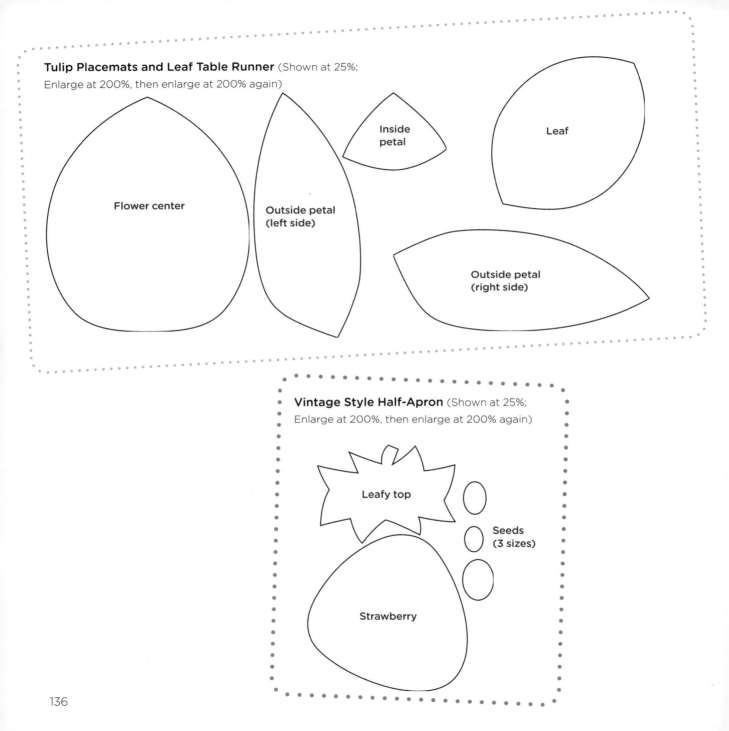

Tulip Placemats and Leaf Table Runner (Shown at 25%; Enlarge at 200%, then enlarge at 200% again)

Flower center

Outside petal (left side)

Inside petal

Leaf

Outside petal (right side)

Vintage Style Half-Apron (Shown at 25%; Enlarge at 200%, then enlarge at 200% again)

Leafy top

Seeds (3 sizes)

Strawberry

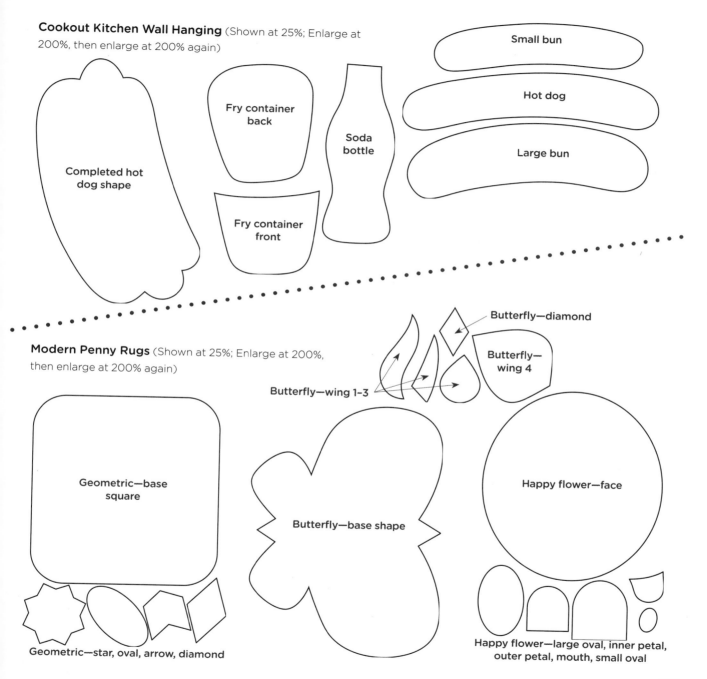

Cookout Kitchen Wall Hanging (Shown at 25%; Enlarge at 200%, then enlarge at 200% again)

Completed hot dog shape

Fry container back

Fry container front

Soda bottle

Small bun

Hot dog

Large bun

Modern Penny Rugs (Shown at 25%; Enlarge at 200%, then enlarge at 200% again)

Butterfly—wing 1–3

Butterfly—diamond

Butterfly—wing 4

Geometric—base square

Butterfly—base shape

Happy flower—face

Geometric—star, oval, arrow, diamond

Happy flower—large oval, inner petal, outer petal, mouth, small oval

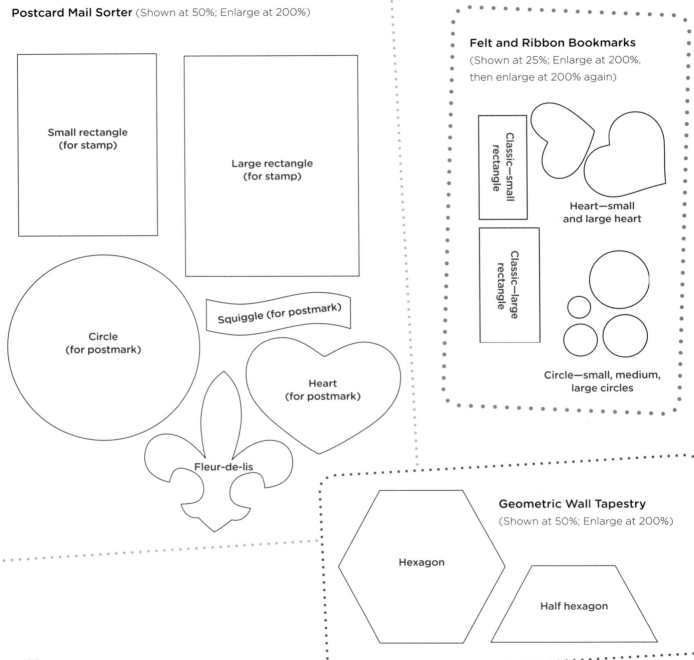

Postcard Mail Sorter (Shown at 50%; Enlarge at 200%)

Small rectangle
(for stamp)

Large rectangle
(for stamp)

Circle
(for postmark)

Squiggle (for postmark)

Heart
(for postmark)

Fleur-de-lis

Felt and Ribbon Bookmarks
(Shown at 25%; Enlarge at 200%,
then enlarge at 200% again)

Classic—small
rectangle

Classic—large
rectangle

Heart—small
and large heart

Circle—small, medium,
large circles

Geometric Wall Tapestry
(Shown at 50%; Enlarge at 200%)

Hexagon

Half hexagon

Embroidered Napkins and Napkin Rings (Shown at 50%; Enlarge at 200%)

Ring circle shape

Cute Cupcake Toppers (Shown at 50%; Enlarge at 200%)

Diamond embroidery design

Flag shape

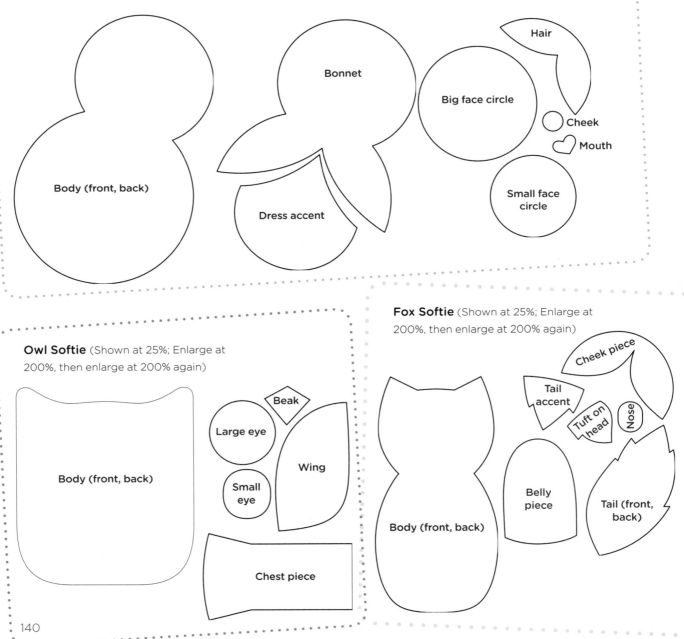

Nesting Doll Softie (Shown at 25%; Enlarge at 200%, then enlarge at 200% again)

Body (front, back)

Bonnet

Dress accent

Big face circle

Small face circle

Hair

Cheek

Mouth

Owl Softie (Shown at 25%; Enlarge at 200%, then enlarge at 200% again)

Body (front, back)

Large eye

Small eye

Beak

Wing

Chest piece

Fox Softie (Shown at 25%; Enlarge at 200%, then enlarge at 200% again)

Body (front, back)

Cheek piece

Tail accent

Tuft on head

Nose

Belly piece

Tail (front, back)

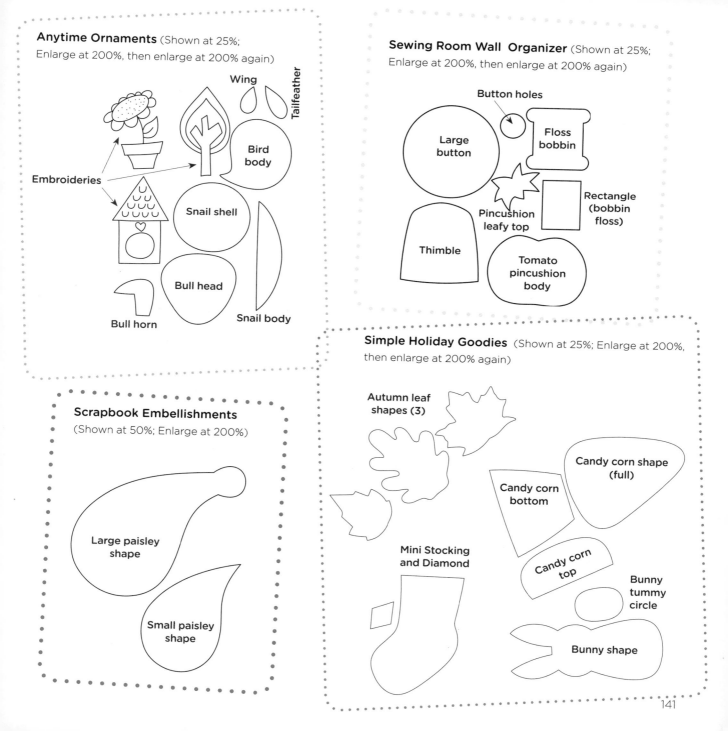

Anytime Ornaments
(Shown at 25%; Enlarge at 200%, then enlarge at 200% again)

Wing

Tailfeather

Bird body

Embroideries

Snail shell

Bull head

Bull horn

Snail body

Sewing Room Wall Organizer
(Shown at 25%; Enlarge at 200%, then enlarge at 200% again)

Button holes

Large button

Floss bobbin

Pincushion leafy top

Rectangle (bobbin floss)

Thimble

Tomato pincushion body

Scrapbook Embellishments
(Shown at 50%; Enlarge at 200%)

Large paisley shape

Small paisley shape

Simple Holiday Goodies
(Shown at 25%; Enlarge at 200%, then enlarge at 200% again)

Autumn leaf shapes (3)

Candy corn shape (full)

Candy corn bottom

Candy corn top

Mini Stocking and Diamond

Bunny tummy circle

Bunny shape

Dedication

To my mom and sister, who always know how to make things special.

Acknowledgments

A super big thank you and hug to all of the lovely people at North Light Books that made this book possible: Kelly, Christine, Jenni, Corrie, Sarah and Greg. Thank you to my super-supportive husband, Joe, for always keeping me happy and telling me that I can do it. Thanks to my family and friends for always being understanding and there to help me cut things out and run to the post office, and for generally being the most awesome people I know. And to all the incredible folks and indie businesses that have supported my work, thank you so much—it means the world to me!

About the Author

Jodie Rackley has always been the artsy-craftsy type. She tried many things, but it was not until she started to embroider that she found her true crafty love. Jodie is known for her bold use of color and the simple designs that comprise her handmade line, Lova Revolutionary.

Her work has been featured on MarthaStewart.com, ApartmentTherapy.com, at the Craft & Hobby Association Trade Show, and in many wonderful boutiques all across the country. She stitches up a storm everyday in her home studio in Fredericksburg, Virginia, where she resides with her husband, Joe, and her sweet little beasts, Captain Nibbles and Sleepy Kitty. She is inspired by modern design both old and new, everything vintage, art and history, music, love, and (of course) handmade. To find out more, or just to stop by and say hello, visit her blog at lovarevolutionary.blogspot.com and on Etsy at lovahandmade.etsy.com.

www.fwmedia.com

16 15 14 13 12   5 4 3 2 1

DISTRIBUTED IN CANADA BY
FRASER DIRECT
100 Armstrong Avenue
Georgetown, ON, Canada L7G 5S4
Tel: (905) 877-4411

DISTRIBUTED IN THE U.K. AND EUROPE
BY F&W MEDIA INTERNATIONAL
Brunel House, Newton Abbot, Devon,
TQ12 4PU, England
Tel: (+44) 1626 323200
Fax: (+44) 1626 323319
E-mail: enquiries@fwmedia.com

DISTRIBUTED IN AUSTRALIA BY
CAPRICORN LINK
P.O. Box 704, S. Windsor NSW, 2756
Australia
Tel: (02) 4577-3555

SRN: W6014
ISBN-13: 978-1-4403-1857-3

Edited by Kelly Biscopink
Designed by Sarah Underhill, Corrie Schaffeld
Production coordinated by Greg Nock
Photographed by Bangwallop Photography, Christine Polomsky, Al Parrish

Index

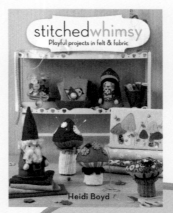